The Journey

Catherine Schubert and Rosa, born on the journey.
(COURTESY OF THE FAMILY)

The Journey

THE OVERLANDERS' QUEST FOR GOLD

Bill Gallaher

TouchWood Editions

Cover and book design by Pat McCallum, layout by Retta Moorman. Cover
illustration NA-1041-9 courtesy of Glenbow Archives, Calgary, AB, cover drawing of
Catherine Schubert courtesy of the family, cover photo of mountains from *Bruno
Engler Photography*, page 103, courtesy of Rocky Mountain Books, Calgary, AB. Maps
by Philip Teece. Chapter-head drawings by Gwen Lewis and Pat McCallum.

We acknowledge the support of The Canada Council for the Arts for our publishing
program. We also wish to acknowledge the financial support of the Government of
Canada through the Book Publishing Industry Development Program (BPDIP) for
our publishing activities. We also acknowledge the financial support of the Province of
British Columbia through the British Columbia Arts Council.
This book is set in Garamond.
Printed and bound in Canada by Friesens, Altona, Manitoba.

National Library of Canada Cataloguing in Publication Data

Gallaher, Bill.
  The journey

  Includes bibliographical references and index.
  ISBN 0-920663-83-4

  1. Overland journeys to the Pacific--Fiction. 2. Northwest,
Canadian--Description and travel--Fiction. 3. Northwest,
Canadian--History--To 1870--Fiction.* I. Title.
PS8563.A424J68 2002   C813'.6   C2002-910478-5
PR9199.4.G34J68 2002

BRITISH
COLUMBIA
ARTS COUNCIL
Supported by the Province of British Columbia

The Canada Council | Le Conseil des Arts
for the Arts | du Canada

Contents

DEDICATION
For Jody and Jennifer

"...made weak by time and fate, but strong in will
to strive, to seek, to find, and not to yield."

Alfred Lord Tennyson, *Ulysses*

ACKNOWLEDGMENTS

Like most books, *The Journey* was not a solitary project. My sincere thanks go to my wife Jaye for her continued support; the staff at the main branch of the Greater Victoria Public Library for their courteous, professional help; Philip Teece for cheerfully doing the map work when he could have been sailing; Marlyn Horsdal, for her expert editorial guidance; and Marlyn and Pat Touchie of TouchWood Editions for once again helping me make our incredible past more accessible to readers.

PROLOGUE

The sound of shattering glass startled Catherine Schubert from her reverie. What on earth had she been thinking of? A thousand things. Nothing. Whatever, it certainly wasn't anything remotely connected to what she was now doing, which was getting drinks for the men gathered in her living room. She placed the wooden tray she was carrying on a nearby table, grabbed the lamp sitting there, and hurried toward the sound that had come from the rear of the house, the bedroom where her infant son James was sleeping. She opened the door and the sight she saw made her heart nearly burst in her chest: an Indian, half naked and painted, with a leg through the window and about to pull the rest of himself inside. With no concern for herself she raced to the bed, skirts flying, swept the child up with one arm and fled from the room, yelling for her husband.

Augustus Schubert was in the living room, which doubled as a tavern, conversing with the customers, when he heard Catherine's call for help, that there was an Indian intruder. He leapt to the blazing fireplace, grabbed an iron poker lying on the hearth, and ran out the front door and around to the back of the house, just

1

as the Indian, a Sioux, hit the ground and stumbled. Augustus swung the poker, catching the intruder across the base of his neck. The Indian had only one thought and that was to get as far away from his attacker as fast as possible, but several more painful blows rained down upon him before he was able to escape into the night.

"I sent him home bruised," Augustus told Catherine. "It'll be a while before he's up to climbing through any more windows."

But the following night a band of 40 Sioux warriors arrived at the front door of the tavern. They were not painted, but some carried rifles and they clearly meant business. They had come seeking retribution for the beating given one of their own, and the payment plan they had in mind included Augustus Schubert. Since this was no time for heroics, Augustus wisely chose to stay inside the house, leaving Catherine to convince the Indians that he wasn't around. When he didn't appear after a few minutes, they left peaceably.

Over the next few days, the family received several death threats, which served to make up their minds. They would head to the colony at Red River, in British territory, north of the 49th parallel. They would rather have avoided such a move, but skirmishes between whites and Indians in the Minnesota Territory in 1860 were becoming a fact of life as settlers pushed westward onto Indian land. Kidnappings had been attempted before in the community around Fort Snelling, where the Schuberts lived, and these acts were not only retaliatory, they were random. So when the men who brought the mail carts down from the colony said that whites and Indians got along much better there, the Schuberts decided to pull up stakes. They quietly sold their house and business, gathered together their three children, as many of their belongings as they could carry and, with two other families sharing similar concerns about the Indians, slipped away in the cold pre-dawn hours, well before the settlement was astir for the coming day's toil.

They led their packhorses northwest along the Mississippi River to St. Cloud, then north to the extensive tracts of conifers that skirted the northeastern edge of the fertile rolling plains, where there were plenty of places to hide should they run into a band of Sioux. The refuge they sought was at the forks of the Red and Assiniboine rivers, 550 miles from Fort Snelling, roughly equivalent to an eternity when winter was breathing ice down the back of one's neck and danger lurked everywhere.

For days they wove their way among stands of pine trees, around swamps, across rivers and past small lakes teeming with geese and ducks until at last they came to the open prairie. Here the land had been sucked dry by the searing summer sun and the grass was brown and brittle. The only trees to be seen were small willows and aspens topping hummocks and lining infrequent streams. The early fall nights were chilly, but at least the mosquitoes and flies were past their season. Formations of geese winging south were lopsided black Vs against the immense backdrop of the sky.

The vast emptiness of the land exposed the refugees more than they liked, and added to their already acute sense of isolation and vulnerability. Entering the Red Lake River valley, a traditional warpath of the Sioux, they were in even greater danger and passed through with much haste. They did not even stop to hunt any of the game birds abundant in the valley for fear that the gunfire would attract Indians. Signs of a recent encampment spurred them on even faster.

The weather was mostly agreeable, but as they neared the Red River floodplain huge black clouds built up on the western horizon with alarming speed, and the wind began to strengthen, throwing grit in their faces and forcing them to seek shelter. They led the animals into a large dry wallow and huddled together as a howling, icy wind roared through. It felt strong enough to pick them up and carry them away. But despite its tremendous force the storm brought only a few snowflakes, none of which stuck to the ground, and by morning it had blown by, leaving a touch of frost and a feel of winter in the air. The travellers spent the night in the wallow and were away early under clearing skies. Nighttime temperatures were now near freezing, but at least it didn't snow, and the weather held all the way to the Red River.

They found an abandoned shack on the river bank that looked to be as good a place as any to spend the night. The men gathered wood and lit a fire, and the women began preparing a meal of beans and jerked beef. They were sitting down to eat when they noticed a dust cloud back in the direction they had just come. There was no telling what it was, except that it probably wasn't a cart train because they would have heard it by now. All they could do was wait and see what it brought.

It was what they feared most, what had brought them to this desolate spot in the first place: Indians, a band of Sioux. The men ordered the women and children inside the shack, while they prepared their rifles and waited. None of them wanted a fight and they hoped they could talk their way out of one.

The Indians rode up, more than a dozen of them. All were painted and all were armed, some carrying old rifles while others held lances. There were more than enough of them to easily overwhelm the men if such was their intention. Luckily, it wasn't.[1] But they were edgy and clearly did not trust the white men. They spoke in their own tongue, and gestured that all they wanted was food and to be on their way. For the men the choice was clear: risk a fight and possibly death by being obstinate, or hand over the few supplies that were left. Despite his fear, Augustus was ready to explode, but wisely kept his temper in check. They gave the Indians all they had, holding back nothing. It wasn't that far to Fort Pembina on the international boundary, so they wouldn't starve. It would help being near the river where there might still be a few ducks around, and if they got nothing, it was better to arrive hungry than to be left where they were, scalpless and an easy dinner for wolves.

Inside the windowless shack the women kept the children close to their sides and cautioned them to be quiet with fingers to their lips. They could hear the horses blowing, the shuffle of restless hooves and the Indians talking. They were terrified. Catherine held James in her arms, rocking him gently so that he would not cry out. She had never felt more defenseless in her life. Surely God would not abandon them here in the middle of nowhere! Her faith refused to accept such a possibility, but she could not stop the trembling in her hands, and her heart seemed to be tripping over itself.

Once the Indians had taken everything they could, they were gone as quickly as they had come, effortlessly crossing the river before disappearing into the western prairie. The women came out of the cabin and joined the men, but the encounter had rendered everyone silent and they had few words to say to each other. So great was their fear of Indians that they couldn't believe they had come away unscathed.

In the morning they did not tarry, and were packed up and gone by first light, hurrying north, as furtive as thieves in their passage to Fort Pembina. There was precious little to eat along the way; even so, they demanded as much from themselves as they did from their horses. At the outpost they purchased enough supplies to see them through to the colony, and three days later, when the stone bastions of Fort Garry appeared on the horizon, the sight was more welcome than anything they might have imagined.

The Schuberts were impressed by the sheer size of the fort and its aura of authority and impregnability. The outlying timbered buildings, on the other hand, left no such impression and seemed more like random piles of stacked wood than a community.

"Doesn't look like much," said Augustus.

"It looks like a fresh start," said Catherine, "and that will have to do."

THE ROAD TO FORT GARRY

Come, let us go, while we are in our prime,
And take the harmless folly of the time!
We shall grow old apace, and die
Before we know our liberty ...
                    Robert Herrick, "Corinna's going a Maying"

St. Catharines to Fort Garry, April 23 — May 26, 1862

Thomas McMicking stood on the platform of the Great Western Railway in St. Catharines, Canada West, surveying the activity around him. He could see his face reflected in the window glass of the train and was not displeased, for he was a handsome man, with wavy black hair and a clean-shaven face that were suggestive more of a dandy than an adventurer. His dark eyes, high forehead and strong jaw reflected intelligence and determination and made him look as serious as he really was.

He could not quite believe what he was about to do: that he was actually going to board this train and allow it to take him on the first leg of a grand journey into the unknown. Thank God, he wasn't alone! Surrounding him were two dozen other men just as eager to share a similar fate, and that by itself eased the feeling that he might very well be stark raving mad. But then again, he mused, perhaps they were all mad; a madness that could be best summed up in one word — gold!

Tales of gold on the far side of the continent had flooded the Canadas for more than three years, rushing like a spring freshet through the hearts of young and old alike and muddying minds that usually ran clear. And despite the tales being mostly tall, they were easily converted into indisputable fact: there was much gold to be had in the undiscovered creeks of British Columbia, gold in such quantities that all a man had to do was stoop down and pick it up. Indeed, many people had already left for the goldfields via Panama, using steamship and rail. Lately, however, an overland route had been touted that led through Rupert's Land to British Columbia, and that was the one McMicking and his companions had chosen. The newspapers were already calling them "overlanders."

If he was anything, McMicking considered himself a sensible man, and he knew that dashing madly off to the wilds of British Columbia wasn't exactly a sensible thing to do. He was also sensitive enough to know that many people held the opinion that he and the others were utter fools. Yet he was filled with an abundance of hope. He was by nature an optimistic man who could find something positive in the direst of circumstances, yet

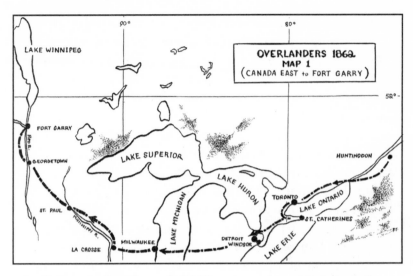

he had never found much fulfillment working his father's farm near Queenston, nor much contentment as a teacher, never mind his brief foray into the business world. Furthermore, he saw Canada West as becoming less and less able to accommodate men of his ilk, men of ambition with a passion to make something of themselves. So this adventure had come along precisely when it was needed. Having just turned 33, he felt it was time for a change in his life — even one as radical as this. Besides, even if there wasn't any gold, he was certain to find numerous opportunities in the new colony of British Columbia.

When he had told his wife, Laura, of his intentions, she had sighed and said, "I can say only that if this is something you feel you need to do for the children and me, then frankly, we would just as soon have you here at home where we know you are all right and we don't have to worry about you. But if it's something you need to do for yourself, then go with our blessing and our prayers."

9

Despite their staunch support, McMicking still wasn't finding it easy leaving his family behind. He would miss them terribly. The rousing send-off earlier that morning in Queenston — it seemed as if the entire community had shown up to wish him and the others well — was nothing short of inspiring but the sorrowful goodbyes to Laura and the children, who did not want to let him go, who would have clung to him forever if their mother hadn't pried them gently away, still lay uneasy in his heart, tainting his excitement with melancholy. But he believed he was doing this as much for them as he was for himself, and if he didn't go now he never would. Once he was established, he would send for them. To a new land, a new life, that's where this train would lead him, lead them all.

He picked up his rifle and suitcase, which was surprisingly light considering the journey in front of him, and boarded the train with his travelling companions. All were similarly bedecked, their suitcases, like McMicking's, probably containing no more than an extra suit of clothes, a few changes of underwear, good socks, knee boots, a rubber coat, one or two blankets, some patent medicines, perhaps even a revolver and a bowie knife. And they too would have their most important possession hidden in a money belt strapped securely around their waist: cash to buy the provisions they would need during the later stages of their long journey overland, after they had left behind the railroad and steamship companies that included food in the price of their tickets.

Huge clouds of smoke and steam billowed up from the engine and roiled back over the passenger cars as the train pulled away from the station in jolting spasms of power, its destination Windsor, slightly more than 200 miles down the line. Off to the right was the empty expanse of Lake Ontario, blue-grey on this overcast day, and to the left, in the distance, was the Niagara escarpment. McMicking took one last, long look, then focussed his attention straight ahead. Though most of his companions had indicated intentions to return after finding their fortunes, for him there would be no reversing his footsteps. As far as he was concerned, he was seeing the last of this part of the world.

Ten hours later the train pulled into Windsor. The men were stiff and sore from the torturous wooden seats, glad to be moving about once more and thankful for the cool fresh air that was like an elixir after the stale air of the train, thick with cigar, cigarette and pipe smoke, sweet perfume and body odour. They were pleased with themselves for having had the foresight to get identification certificates from the Custom House at Queenston, for it allowed them to cross easily over onto American soil without interruption.

To McMicking, Detroit seemed bursting with people, Some 47,000 of them called the city home and far too many were dressed in soldiers' uniforms, awaiting dispatch to some tragic battle against the Confederacy.[1] He sensed a measure of relief when, on the following morning, the train left the city behind, swaying past endless orchards ready to bloom, and farms with grazing cattle. In front of him and his companions were ten more hours of sitting on seats that rivalled those of the Great Western in their ability to inflict pain on the human posterior. But at a top speed of 30 miles per hour, and an average of 19, no other form of land transportation was as speedy. To them, they were figuratively flying across the peninsula to Grand Haven on the Lake Michigan shore, and for that, they were grateful.

At Grand Haven, they switched immediately to the steamer *Detroit* which rumbled away from the dock well after dark, pitching and rolling across the rough lake toward Milwaukee.

Several of the men spent the five-hour passage with their heads over the rails and their guts heaving more boisterously than the white-capped waters below. The ship's movement didn't bother McMicking, who joined a few of his companions in the saloon for a couple of brandies. Later, he found a quiet spot where he was able to put his feet up and reflect on the day. All of a sudden he was in the water, being pulled down into the deep, black silence by some powerful force from which he could not escape. He struggled to kick free, but could not move his legs. He tried to claw his way upward, but the light above only grew dimmer. He held his breath until he could hold it no longer, and he had no choice but to breathe in. As the water flowed into his nose and mouth he woke up, choking, trying to catch his breath. For an instant he feared that the ship had foundered, but his surroundings told him otherwise. It was only a bad dream. Yet it had seemed very real for he could not remember falling asleep. He had been sitting there thinking about the day's journey, and the next thing he knew he was drowning. It disturbed him enough that he returned to the saloon and ordered another brandy.

At two in the morning the ferry reached Milwaukee where the men stopped over till supper time. This allowed those who were ill to recover for the rail journey to La Crosse, a small town on the Mississippi River, and another 200 miles deeper into the west.

Up to that point, the trip had gone quite smoothly, better than McMicking had expected, but after Milwaukee, things began to decline. The train was delayed for eight hours at Portage City because the spring freshets on the Wisconsin River had washed out the track. To reduce the weight of the train, passengers had to carry their own baggage across a temporary trestle. There was water everywhere, and once the train was across and under way again, the next seven or eight miles were like travelling across a vast lake. They crawled down a long valley between low craggy hills, then passed through a mile-long tunnel, black and dripping with water. By the time they reached La Crosse it had taken them an exhausting 29 hours to cover the 200 miles from Milwaukee. And they would soon find out, on the journey up the flooded Mississippi to St. Paul, that things could get even worse.

Before leaving Queenston, McMicking had worked out a deal with the railway company by which he guaranteed a minimum of 20 through passengers to St. Paul in exchange for first-class tickets at second-class rates. Indeed, his party numbered 24, and for the most part, the contract had been honoured and the men treated well. But when they boarded the side-wheel packet *Frank Steel,* they were put between decks without a place to stretch out and sleep, and worse, the service and food were abominable. That might not have been so bad if the steamer had made its run in the scheduled time, but there were endless delays up the capricious river and it arrived in St. Paul some 24 hours late. The only redeeming part of the entire trip was that they had passed the steamer *Northern Belle,* laid up by engine problems. Many of her passengers were also men from the Canadas bound for the goldfields, and the two groups saluted each other with loud cheers and rifle volleys.

Otherwise, it had been the most miserable part of the trip. McMicking complained to the officers, but to no avail. This was, after all, the very edge of the frontier, and he was perfunctorily told that he might as well get used to it because things were bound to get a lot worse before they got better. But that was not the issue for McMicking. He expected his creature comforts to decline the farther west he got, and that the road ahead would only get rougher

— the "road," in this case, meaning simply a "course" or a "path," nothing more than the patch of ground a person was moving on. Yet that was a part of the adventure of it all. He just hadn't expected it to happen so soon. It made him angry, for he was a man of his word and expected others to respond in kind. Nevertheless, it was his custom to control such emotions, so he generously offered to pay extra to obtain the amenities promised him back in Queenston. His pleas fell on ears dulled by having heard such complaints too many times before. He seethed inside, but said nothing more. To do so would be to step outside the boundaries within which a gentleman must always conduct himself.

St. Paul had come a long way from its dubious beginnings some 20 years earlier when it was a single cabin owned by one Pierre "Pig's-Eye" Parrant, who made his living selling liquor to soldiers from a nearby fort, as well as to the Indians. It was an ideal site on which to build a community. There was a fresh-water creek on one side of the cabin and a river highway in front, and the fort provided settlers with a measure of security. Given the great movement of people westward it wasn't long before more cabins began springing up. The place was known as "Pig's-Eye" until a cleric came along and gave a sermon so inspiring that the citizenry, in a stunning leap of the imagination, promptly changed its name to St. Paul. It sat now on both banks of the Mississippi against a backdrop of rolling hills, with the winter-beaten prairie spreading away around it. The town on the west bank was completely flooded and deserted, but the eastern town-site (now Minneapolis) sat at a higher elevation and was dry and free of the swollen river. The population had grown to almost 11,000 people, many of whom were merchants awaiting the arrival of the overlanders as eagerly as a child awaits Christmas.

A spring bloom of new stone and wooden buildings was unfolding, and the town was busy now that the river was relatively free of ice and steamers were beginning to arrive. Like the McMicking party, many of the people flooding the streets were transients on their way to discover some great fortune. The word around town was that there wouldn't be much to choose from in the way of supplies if they waited to purchase them at Fort Garry, so there was a buying frenzy as the Queenston men amassed most of what they would need for the remainder of their journey. They bought gunpowder, caps, lead for bullets and bags of shot. Hardware items included nails, axes, scythes, picks, shovels, rope, matches, needles with twine, cooking utensils and a baking oven. For food there was salted ham, beans, biscuits, tea, coffee, ginger, tartar and baking powder. Finally, they bought tents, which were simply pieces of tarpaulin that had to be sewn together. The men immediately set about doing this, but it proved to be a chore they would have to repeat over and over again, for the seams would leak like cheesecloth, even in the most modest of rainfalls.

They also attended a meeting with other groups from the Canadas; everyone seemed to recognize that there was strength in numbers, and that they would be far better off co-operating with each other than competing. So they formed a loose association, held together by a thin glue of common goals and common sense.

The next leg of the journey was overland by stage to Georgetown on the Red River, then by steamer to Fort Garry. McMicking baulked at the through fare — $35 — for it was a distance of only 600 miles compared to the 900 he had just come from Queenston, and for which he had paid a mere $16.65. But it was fast becoming apparent that everything on the frontier was expensive, including travel. Regardless, the news did not sit well with McMicking whose Scottish-Presbyterian frugality rose to the occasion. He bargained with the stage-line owners until they relented and reduced the fare to $25.

There was another disappointment. His inquiries back home about the transportation facilities between St. Paul and Georgetown had led him to believe that the vehicles used by the stage-line were in fact coaches. Instead, they were only canvas-covered freight wagons jammed to capacity with people and goods, and sometimes even a dog or two. There was nothing to be done about it. The path was laid out before him now and he either travelled down it or retreated. And retreating was not on his agenda.

The wagons were well spread out as they made their way up the road. At first they passed farmers sowing the first crops of the season, then the farther north they went the colder it got until the surrounding hillsides were patched with snow and some of the lakes were laced with ice. The bridge at St. Cloud had been washed out, which necessitated crossing the Mississippi by ferry. As they turned westward, houses along the road became fewer until there were none, and the country opened up into low rolling hills and sporadic thickets of scrub trees. The road was sandy and full of axle-deep holes that caught the freight wagons up from time to time, but with the horses pulling and the men pushing, they came out easily enough. Eventually the land became featureless and table-flat, and the only obstacles in their way were the numerous streams that had to be crossed. McMicking was surprised to discover that the town of Breckenridge, on the Red River, consisted of just two buildings, when his map clearly showed it as a city with many streets and parks. Even Fort Abercrombie, several miles up the road, was a major disappointment. They had hoped to find a proper settlement there but it was just a destitute fort, not capable of fulfilling even its frontline role of keeping the Indians in check. (This would soon become apparent in the summer, as the Sioux swept down on some of the nearby settlements and even attacked the very wagon McMicking was riding on, killing and scalping the passengers and driver before dumping the stage unceremoniously into the river.[1]) Still, there was a spirit of high adventure amongst the men that evoked much singing and laughter over the six days that it took to jounce and joggle over the rough trail to Georgetown.

More a village than a town, Georgetown didn't offer much that was pleasing to the eye. One traveller called it a miserable hole that only existed because it was at the head of navigation on the river, as far up as a boat of good size could go. There were a couple of small log houses, some teepees, an HBC storehouse, a factor's residence, a barracks for about three dozen American soldiers and, best of all, a tavern which was soon filled with gold seekers. Tents were pitched and fires kindled, and smoke from the green wood hung like dirty white wool in the barren branches overhead. The community was a desolate sight there amongst the dormant trees, on mud-stricken ground, but no one cared very much. They didn't expect to be there long, but as things turned out, it would be their home for nearly two weeks.

The steamer *International,* which was supposed to depart for Fort Garry in two days — May 10 — was not ready, and wouldn't be for a while. Such news, though disappointing, was no longer surprising, and the men accepted it stoically. A few, who were too impatient to wait, struck out in canoes. Alexander Dallas, who was on his way to take over as governor of Rupert's Land and couldn't afford to wait, was about to set out for the colony on horseback. Before he left, McMicking cleverly brought him on side.

Dallas and his family were staying at the factor's residence, so McMicking formed his party into two ranks, marched them to the residence and saluted him with a volley of rifle shots. The governor-to-be was pleased that his importance was recognized in that obscure outpost on the edge of nowhere. With much ceremony he thanked McMicking, promising him and his men all the help and protection they would need once they reached British territory. After several rousing cheers for Dallas, Queen Victoria, President Lincoln, even Dallas' wife, who was a daughter of James Douglas, the men marched off, their voices raised in a stirring delivery of "God Save the Queen."

Later, McMicking was accosted by James Sellar, a young man whom he'd met briefly in St. Paul; he had arrived there with a party of 19 men from Huntingdon, in Canada East. Indeed, they had been on the *Northern Belle* when McMicking and the other Queenston men had passed it on the *Frank Steele*. Sellar was tall, in his mid-twenties, but looked older with deep-set eyes and a pinched face partially hidden by a bushy black beard. He said he'd worked on his father's farm back in Huntingdon, but knew he was destined for something greater. All he had to do was to go out and find it. He was fidgety, a talker, a man who needed to fill every waking minute of the day with some kind of activity. McMicking sensed he would be difficult to keep up with. Indeed, he had just walked 275 miles, from St. Paul to Georgetown, after refusing to pay the exorbitant stage price of $35 for each man and his supplies. Instead, for $150 the party hired a wagon to haul their freight, and walked. Sellar had left most of his companions behind, averaging more than 30 miles a day. His feet were killing him, he said uncomplainingly, and at one point he had to walk on tiptoe because he had so many blisters. But as far as he knew, the *International* would sail at its scheduled departure time and he was determined not to miss it.

"It appears you needn't have hurried," said McMicking blandly, despite being impressed by Sellar's accomplishment.

Sellar chuckled. He liked McMicking. The man's intelligence and competence were obvious, but it was the salute to Dallas that impressed him most. He didn't doubt that McMicking's actions were sincere, but believed they were not without a small measure of artifice. "It's a wise man who always plans ahead," he said, to which McMicking merely smiled.

Nearly a week passed and the *International* was still not fit for travel. Each day saw the arrival of more gold seekers, and the woods around Georgetown became crowded with tents and men. They soon grew tired of waiting, tired of days sitting on their hands, nights of drinking, fiddling, singing and dancing with each other around campfires that were more smoke than fire. They were also tired of fearing Indian attacks. A band of warriors had been by, demanding payment from the captain for permission to ply their river, as well as for the firewood the vessel would use. Nothing came of it, but everyone was restless and anxious to move on. A delegation of overlanders, headed by McMicking, complained to the *International*'s captain.

Captain Cornelius Lull was a reasonable man and offered to supply some pemmican for the remainder of the waiting time. The mainstay of those who regularly traversed the plains, pemmican was buffalo meat cut into thin strips, partially cooked, then sun- or smoke-dried, after which it was pounded into powder and mixed with fat rendered from the skin. Then berries, usually saskatoons, were added. The nourishing mixture would keep for years, and the vitamin C content provided by the berries helped prevent scurvy during winter months. Nevertheless, hunger was said to be the best sauce for it.

Lull also suggested that instead of grumbling, the men might do better by putting their backs into getting the steamer ready for sailing. Some of the men thought the idea preposterous. Hadn't they already paid for their passage? Why should they now have to work for it? However, McMicking recognized that these were unusual circumstances. He repeated to the others what he himself had been told back on the Mississippi. "This is the frontier," he added, "and if this boat doesn't get going we will either have to walk to Fort Garry or turn back. You can decide for yourselves, but I know what's required of me."

The spring air was soon filled with the din of labour as most of the men pitched in to prepare the *International* for departure. At noon on May 20, she was ready for boarding.

The Huntingdon men were frustrated. They had appointed a delegation in St. Cloud to buy some oxen and carts, thinking that they would be much cheaper there than in Fort Garry. Now Captain Lull was telling them that he did not have room for the animals, because far more people had showed up for ship's run north than he had expected. The men held a meeting and decided to take the animals overland to Fort Garry, rather than wait for the ship to return for its next trip. Any number of things could happen to delay it. Sellar, who had never felt more fit in his life after the march from St. Paul, volunteered to do it. A few others joined him. They bought themselves riding horses and pack mules, and with the oxen, swam them across the river to an old cart trail that led to the fort, more than 200 miles distant. Then they ferried their carts and supplies across and set up camp. In the morning, after thinking about it for much of the night, Sellar went back to Georgetown and hired a guide. He said farewell to his friends again, wishing them God speed, then returned to the west bank to begin the long trek north.

Meanwhile, the air was as heavy with rain as it was with anticipation and excitement while the last of the passengers boarded the *International*. In addition to the 150 or so overlanders, there were Mrs. Dallas and Bishop Alexander Taché, who was returning to the colony at Red River after an extended absence in Europe. The men left behind to wait for the next sailing lined the shore and cheered as the steamer's lines were cast off and she pulled away from the dock with a blast of her whistle.

The *International* was a stern-wheeler, 134 feet long and 26 feet on her beam, and moved awkwardly as she picked up speed down the narrow channel. Muddy bow waves rushed to each shore and set the bushes there swaying so that they too seemed to be acknowledging the big vessel's departure. With each gust of wind, thousands of sparks from the ship's furnaces flew along the lower deck, lodging in the beams and singeing the wood. (During the journey, these areas would have to be soaked with buckets of water to prevent them from catching on fire.) The Red was running high and silt-laden, and overhanging trees sometimes tore at the steamer's top deck; the current, though strong, was mostly in her favour. She had been delayed far too long getting ready for her first voyage of the season to Fort Garry and the passengers' patience had been severely tried. They hoped that was all in the past now that she was under way. The relief and excitement aboard were palpable — and about to be put to the test.

Two miles down river, the captain lost control of the helm and the steamer drifted toward shore. Branches of the tall trees lining the bank toppled her twin smokestacks, scarred her paint and cracked one of the pilothouse windows. The passengers groaned, and some even jeered. It took the rest of the day and part of the following morning to complete repairs. At ten o'clock her steam was up again, but at three o'clock the engine died. By the time it was revived there was only enough light left to run a few miles before tying up for the night. Similar delays marked their passage down the river and many passengers were beginning to wonder if the ship would ever make Fort Garry. A handful were threatening to get off and walk.

The next two days were relatively uneventful and the men began to relax a little and enjoy the voyage. Many lazed around the boat playing cards while a few vied for the attention of Mrs. Dallas and Bishop Taché. There was not much to see to the right or to the left, except trees, and prairie in the spaces between them. The scenery grew tedious and the trip boring until several Canadian passengers requested that the captain fly the Union Jack to honour Queen Victoria's birthday. He adamantly refused. Addressing the contingent that had gathered on the bridge, he said, "May I remind you, gentlemen, that the ship is still in American territory. The British flag is reserved for north of the international boundary. To fly it before then would be an insult."

"It would be a greater insult not to honour our queen!" said one of the more ardent Canadians, and with that he led the men to the pole, lowered the American flag, and ran up an old rag. They guarded the pole so that the ship's crew couldn't get near. Finally Captain Lull acceded to the small mutiny, and brought out the Union Jack. When it was snapping in the wind, the men celebrated with shouts of "God save the Queen" and a thunderous rifle volley, followed by the anthem and several extemporaneous speeches. McMicking had never felt more proud to be Canadian than he did at that moment. He was convinced that the incident was proof beyond all doubt of their deep attachment to the Gracious Sovereign under *all* circumstances. There followed enough generous toasts to the queen's good health to ensure that more than a few Canadians were laid low the following morning.

Early the next day they discovered that their bad luck had only taken a hiatus. The rudder broke, and with the ship so far behind schedule that food was running low, passengers were rationed to two meals a day, mostly salt pork and beans. Complaints flew back and forth from one end of the boat to the other and in a petulant fit, one man threw his ration overboard, declaring he'd rather go hungry. This was not the kind of behaviour that Lull understood. Anyone who would throw out perfectly good pork and beans had obviously not yet tasted pemmican, which was next on the menu if the ship experienced any further delays. Besides, how was he to know that so many people would show up at Georgetown expecting passage north?

As the *International* neared Fort Pembina, it was greeted by a less than friendly band of Indians. They lined the riverbank, waving their ancient rifles and firing them into the air. The passengers responded to the threatening gesture in kind, firing a volley from their own heavy calibre, more modern guns. The vessel slipped by, leaving a pall of gun smoke hanging over the river. When she tied up for the night at the fort, Captain Lull was concerned enough to post a watch schedule. There was no shortage of volunteers. Later that evening a few drunken Indians actually tried to board the vessel but they changed their minds when they saw how well armed the passengers were. There was a brief standoff, with both sides posturing, and then the Indians disappeared into the dark. The rest of the night passed quietly.

A day or so later they were only 50 miles south of Fort Garry, as a crow flies. By water, they were more than twice that distance. The river was so serpentine that the ship's bow swung constantly from east through north to west then back through north to east again. So seldom was it pointed in a northerly direction it was difficult to tell that that was the direction they were actually seeking. It was slow going, and those who needed to quell their appetites were eating biscuits and pemmican that was mouldy and full of buffalo hairs. By late afternoon, Fort Garry was sighted on the horizon and the passengers let out a cheer. By supper time Lull was shutting down the *International's* steam as she rounded the point into the Assiniboine River, bumping into the shallows of the north shore before coasting to a landing in front of the stone walls of the fort. A journey that usually took only two days had taken nearly a week.

A large crowd had gathered along the bank to greet the ship, cheering the arrival of the overlanders and the steamer's successful inaugural run. The passengers fired a volley of shots in reply. McMicking, lost in reverie, paid scant attention. His mind's eye saw beyond the fort and its amenities, to the great emptiness beyond. Despite the discomforts they had all had to contend with — the fatigue-inducing train seats, the interminable delays, the hardscrabble camps and the finicky steamers — he knew that compared to what lay ahead they had had a relatively easy passage so far. Out there, somewhere beneath the lowering sun, was where the real adventure awaited them all. He felt something large roll over in his gut.

THE ROAD TO FORT EDMONTON

I see the grass shake in the sun for leagues on either hand,
I see a river loop and run about a treeless land —
An empty plain, a steely pond, a distance diamond-clear,
And low blue naked hills beyond. And what is that to fear?
Rudyard Kipling, "The Prairie"

FORT GARRY TO FORT EDMONTON, MAY 27 — JULY 25, 1862

The big stone fort covered about four acres. Its massive walls were twelve feet high and four feet thick with impressive circular bastions marking each of its four corners. Inside the enclosure was a collection of wooden buildings ranging from the governor's residence to storehouses. From the outside, it looked staid and solemn, and it seemed to brood over the community beside it like a mare over a wayward foal.

In addition to the fort, the colony included about 50 sawn-timber buildings, mostly mud-plastered so that they looked unkempt and uncared for. Except for the churches, that is, of which there were several. There were no streets to speak of, just a hodgepodge of rutted tracks concocted in the infernal mud of spring and baked hard in the oven of summer, through which carts and wagons pulled by draft animals creaked and moaned. There was always the smell of something in the air: smoke, manure, garbage, even human waste.

On the eastern shore a stone cathedral was under construction and not far away was a large white building of two storeys and a steeply pitched roof that served as a nunnery. Other buildings were scattered about.

The agricultural settlement actually stretched for nearly 30 miles up and down both sides of the river from the fort, and more than 20 miles west along both banks of the Assiniboine. This was largely due to the way the Métis allotted land, which was patterned after the French-Canadian seigneurial system. The lots were long and narrow, and provided river frontage for everyone, as well as the security of having neighbours close by. The land was as arable as any McMicking had seen, but, except for grazing livestock, remarkably underused.[1] As near as he could tell, the farming was largely subsistence, mostly Indian corn, hay and wheat. All the place needed, he reckoned, was a market, a very large market, and there'd be no problems supplying it with the necessary produce.

Several thousand people lived here, of a variety of different cultures. A slim majority were Métis, descendants of French-Canadian

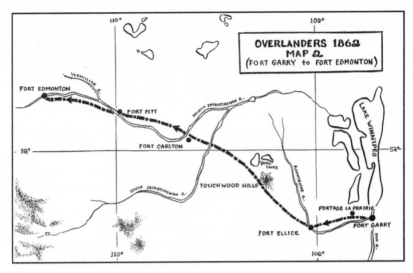

voyageurs and native women, and the rest were whites, Indians, and others of mixed heritage, mostly of Scottish and native descent and commonly referred to as cross-breeds, half-breeds or country-born. This diverse community was held together by the delicate threads of commerce. It was commerce that made it work, that provided its foundation and a common point at which to meet. Without it, reconciling the cultural differences that separated the people would probably have been impossible.

The Hudson's Bay Company fort was the administrative and economic hub, and reflected the power of the Company over the northern plains, a power it had enjoyed for nearly two centuries. But tendrils of change were creeping through the community that would ultimately strangle the Company's monopoly. Immigrants, who would swell the population of this area over time, trading old ways for new, would see to it. The

Company did not appreciate in the least these threats to its existence, but it would be powerless to do anything about it.

The gold seekers pitched their tents in an orderly fashion east of the fort, near the point of land where the Assiniboine and Red rivers met. Then those who hadn't already done so in St. Paul went about buying the things they would need to see them through to Cariboo. The factor had never experienced such a rush on the Company's stores and was worried that supplies would run low for the community. So were some of the settlers. However, Governor Dallas had not forgotten the promise he had made to McMicking in Georgetown, and goods were passed over the counter as fast as the men could lay down their money. Dallas had also promised not to raise prices because of the heavy demand and kept his word in that regard too, but said he had no control beyond the walls of the fort. Nevertheless, by fixing the Company's prices, he limited the prices merchants in the settlement could charge. None of them were happy with these circumstances. If the overlanders saw gold in their dreams, the merchants saw gold in the overlanders and wanted to raise their prices accordingly. It was just another blow to the wedge already driven deeply between the Company and the local merchants.

McMicking found the prices excessive, but few were as good as he when it came to nose-to-nose bargaining. He got an ox for $30, and his horse for $40, while most of the others paid as high as $50 for an ox and $100 for a horse. Red River carts were selling anywhere from $10 to $20, but McMicking got his for $8.

The carts were odd-looking contraptions, and he wished that conventional four-wheel wagons were available, even though they might have been more expensive. But carts were the way things were moved on the prairies, and those with experience wouldn't have it any other way. This fact was most obvious by their presence — the carts were everywhere, as vital to the land as a canoe was to water. And like the canoe, they were truly a product of their environment.

Made entirely of wood, there was not a nail to be found in them anywhere. The sides and bottom of the box were held together by dowels, and even the wheel rims were wooden. The wheels themselves were deliberately over-sized — more than five feet in diameter — which prevented frequent overturning, kept the box high off rough terrain and allowed room for sleeping beneath it. The rims were wrapped in wet rawhide that acted as a primitive form of tire when it dried. The axles were wooden and fit into the wheel hub with no metal attachments whatsoever. Grease was rarely used because dirt and dust got into it and bound the wheels to the axle, yet without grease the wheels emitted a hellish shriek that could be heard for miles and gave the cart its other name — the "Northwest Fiddle." This noise was the cart's only real disadvantage. Because they contained no metal, they were light and easy to lift out of mud holes. If a cart broke down along the trail, it could easily be repaired with wood from trees that lined the frequent rivers and streams. Best of all, when those same rivers and streams had to be crossed, the wheels could be removed and placed inside the box, or attached on the outside or bottom, and the unwieldy thing paddled to the opposite shore like a square canoe. Thus far, no invention had proved as useful to a prairie traveller as the Red River cart.

Few of the overlanders were impressed, however, and made jokes about the carts even as they bought them for the journey west. They wouldn't be too far along the trail before the true worth of the vehicles would be realized.

By the time the final purchases were made the men had amassed a mountain of goods. The basic provisions required for each group of five included 400 pounds of pemmican, 700 of flour, and 30 of tea, as well as beans, dried codfish, dried apples and smoked bacon in slabs. Adding to the pile were sundry items ranging from clothes and water casks to shotguns and coffeepots. To carry all this, the same five-man group would need four carts, four horses and three oxen. Those who could afford it bought horses for riding. Those who couldn't bought extra shoes.

While it was easy to buy a good pair of shoes, horses were a different matter. Most of the men had little or no experience with the animals and therefore had no inkling of what they should be looking for. Few knew, for example, that a horse's age and general health could be determined simply by checking its teeth. Instead, they based their decision on the appearance of the horse, or if it could run fast — both poor measurements of the animal's ability to pull a cart loaded with several hundred pounds of goods. But the trail was waiting, and it would let them know soon enough about the decisions they had made.

There was such a buzz of gold around the settlement that no one failed to hear it. Few were more excited by it than Augustus Schubert. Since the place had begun filling with men on their way west to seek their fortunes he had heard the talk and drunk in the rumours the way some of his patrons poured whiskey down their throats, and he knew that his fortune also awaited him among the lofty mountains of British Columbia.

He concluded that he should go on his own and leave Catherine and the children behind in the settlement. Had they not already journeyed far enough for the time being? Had the children's lives not been disrupted enough? Placed at risk enough? Not only that, there was now something else that must be considered, something even more important. Catherine was four months pregnant. For that reason alone it wouldn't be wise to undertake a long and arduous journey to the goldfields. It would be best to send for her and the children when his fortune was a *fait accompli*.

He put his case to Catherine who ached to interrupt him several times but patiently heard him out. When he was done there wasn't a hair's breadth between his last word and her first.

"So it's leaving us behind that you're thinking of, is it, Gus? Me waiting here with a saint's patience and a bride-of-Christ's loyalty for your beck and call while you go traipsing over the horizon in a cloud of dust! And when the time comes for us to join you — praise God if we're all still alive — what if no more cart trains go seeking the west?[2] Where might that be leaving us, do you think? Would you be having me and the children take the Oregon Trail, only to be savaged by Indians who for good reason have not exactly taken a liking to white folks, and where every man carries a pistol in one pocket and a flask of whiskey in the other? Or is having us sail halfway around the world in leaky ships what you're proposing? You, of all people, know that I have sailed across one ocean already and would not care to sail across another, thank you just the same. I know your intentions are wholesome, Gus, but you've never been a fool and this is no time to start working on it. You'll not be leaving here without your family, and that's the way of it."

There were other sound reasons for all of them to leave together. Both of the Schuberts were disappointed with the way things had gone for them in the colony, indeed with life on the prairies in general.

It hadn't taken long to settle once they arrived in the colony. The business of starting from scratch was familiar and they soon opened a roadhouse on a farm on the east side of the Red River, not far from the cathedral and the nunnery. As a Catholic, Catherine found comfort in the fact that a large papist population lived here.[3] Granted, they were mostly Métis, but she felt the substance of their faith and was reassured in her own. Besides, she sometimes thought that being Catholic and Irish was only a small step up the social ladder from having mixed blood.

Initially, life moved along reasonably well, but then a series of small disasters befell them. Much to their chagrin, they and the roadhouse made the local newspaper when a customer drank himself into a stupor and died in one of their beds. This did little for their reputation as hosts and there was a subsequent loss of business. In the spring of 1861, the Red River flooded its banks, not as disastrously as in previous years, but bad enough that it all but drowned their house, not to mention their business. Weeks passed before they were able to get started again and the high-water mark that remained on some of the buildings was a worrisome reminder that nature was always in control here. Then in the high heat of summer they were robbed. Indians broke into the roadhouse and stole ten gallons of whiskey along with some household items. They didn't know who the culprits were, and could do nothing about it. Augustus was outraged.

Now, the future didn't look much brighter. They could clearly see that all was not well in the settlement. Political and racial unrest smouldered beneath the relatively placid surface of everyday commerce. Not only was a struggle for power developing, relationships between the various ethnic groups were deteriorating, and there was no telling where it all would lead. Best to get out now while the opportunity presented itself. The children were resilient enough to handle it, and insofar as Catherine's pregnancy was concerned, Augustus hoped it wouldn't be a problem. With any luck at all, they would reach British Columbia long before the baby was due. If not, well, if Métis and Indian women were tough enough to give birth on the trail, then so was Catherine.

The Schuberts easily sold off their business and all the possessions they couldn't take with them. Later, Augustus found himself across the river on a buying spree of his own, acquiring food, an ox, a milk cow, so that the children would not be without milk, and horses, including a sturdy buckskin mare for Catherine. His final purchase was two basket cradles that could be slung over the mare's withers, one for Mary Jane, who would soon turn four, and the other for two-year-old James. Augustus Jr., now six years old, would ride with his father. Instead of spending money on a cart they would use the spring democrat wagon they had purchased to haul spirits to their roadhouse.[4] The ox and the milk cow would make good yoke-mates.

Over the course of the next few days he spoke to a few of the overlanders about joining the train and most seemed indifferent. It wasn't their decision; indeed, it was no one's decision. There was no formal structure to the proposed train, they said; it wouldn't be anything more than a collection of people with the same goal in mind. He could join if wanted, and if others didn't like it, they would soon let him know.

About 150 gold seekers were now gathered in the settlement. They hailed from various parts of the Canadas and came in parties named after their hometowns. Most were as small as six or seven men, but there were three large groups of approximately two dozen each. These were McMicking's Queenston party, Sellar's Huntingdon party, and another from St. Thomas, a small town south of London. All still agreed to the loose association they had discussed in St. Paul. They would be far better off as a company, pooling their resources and skills, than fragmented and possibly at odds with each other.

Sellar had also arrived in the settlement, only three days after the *International*, none the worse for wear and proud of accomplishing the journey with such speed. McMicking ran across him in the campsite and insisted on hearing the details of his journey. It would give him some indication of what the rest of them were about to face.

They had made good time, Sellar told him, all things given due consideration, and even had a hearty laugh when they passed the *International* broken down on the river. For the most part the trail was good, and from what he'd been led to understand, a whole lot better than the one they were about to embark upon. They had spent the first day travelling through several inches of water, but as elevation was gained at the edge of the floodplain, the trail began to dry out, and they set a no-nonsense, determined pace with Sellar leading the way. For every step that the water had slowed them down they took two quick ones on dry land to make up for it. With the good weather it was easy to pick up the pace, for the trail ran straight and true, mile after mile, across a grassy plain as flat as a lake. If there was a tree anywhere about, there was no one with the eyesight to spot it.

Four days out and the horizon was as vacant as it had been the day before, and the day before that. All they had seen was an abandoned Indian tent, with a wooden cask and traps lying outside, and they could only surmise that some horrible fate had befallen the owner. Early the next morning they crossed a river, with the sun bright and warm on the eastern horizon, the sky cloudless, and the wind not yet asserting its dominion over the land. Sellar was the first to spot the unusual shapes where the trail ahead disappeared into the immensity of the sky. As near as he could tell they were not human; rather they were angular and hard, like boulders cast there by some giant hand. Slowly, the gap closed; the men didn't speak. The eerily still air amplified the familiar sound of their cart wheels grinding on axles, the creaking of leather, the lowing of oxen, the snuffling of a horse. Closer now, and Sellar could see that the shapes were not boulders at all, but carts, Red River carts, battered and scattered helter-skelter along the trail. In the long shadows of the morning it was a ghostly scene, and now he could see the mounds of graves, human graves, not in ordered rows as in a cemetery but chaotic, people buried where they had died. It was such a haunting, almost surrealistic sight out there in the middle of nowhere that Sellar shuddered, as if Death had run an icy finger down his spine.

"They're Indian graves," the guide said. "Sioux. Three hundred of them attacked a Métis buffalo-hunting party and came out at the wrong end of a four-hour battle. When the smoke cleared,

96 Indians were dead. Believe it or not, the Métis lost only one man, but they lost all their stock and that's the reason the carts were left behind. I know it doesn't look it, but it happened nine years ago."

Sellar was stunned by that last piece of information. "You'd swear it happened only recently!"

"Well, we'll all live longer if we pretend that it did. Letting your guard down in this country can be a fatal mistake."

While gathering up some boards from the wrecked carts for firewood, Sellar found a small, tarnished silver spoon that he kept as a souvenir — a reminder that when Death came calling, you usually didn't know he was even in the neighbourhood.

Later, they traversed a series of rocky ridges so rough that the carts were upset several times, their contents thrown every which way. Sellar begrudged every moment it took to right them again. They crossed a lake-sized slough, perhaps a remnant of the flood of 1861, and splashed through water a foot deep for three miles. That the carts didn't get mired down was a small miracle. On the far side, a black bear appeared suddenly, sending the oxen into a frenzy. They upset the carts, tore out of their harnesses and ran onto the prairie, eyes wide with fear. After the men chased the bear off, it took them the best part of an hour to restore order and get under way again.

Other than the bear, they hadn't seen much wildlife on the journey, just some ducks and geese on the slough, a line of milk-white swans gracing a mud-brown stream, killdeer with their strange cry, hawks gliding on thermals and a variety of other birds including blue herons and cranes and some for which the men had no names. But after sighting the bear they began to catch glimpses of other animals: antelopes with their white rumps disappearing over a rise, and plenty of elk tracks, though they failed to spot any elk. They even saw a couple of prairie wolves, as scrawny as anything they had ever laid eyes on.

In their need to gain Fort Garry, the group travelled on Sunday, which Sellar hated. He was a pious man and to him Sunday belonged to the Lord. It was a day to stay put, rest up, and give thanks; in fact, he had hurried the party along for exactly that reason, so they would have time to lie up. He let his feelings be known, and a heated discussion followed, but he was completely outnumbered. He could either go along with the majority or stay behind, alone. Though set in his ways, Sellar was no fool. He saddled up his horse, annoyed yet strangely satisfied that democracy had run its due course there in that boundless wilderness.

The trail became indistinct. They seemed to have branched off the main one, into the low rises of the Pembina Mountains; nevertheless, the guide assured them that the town of St. Joseph was just a couple of miles farther on. Sellar suggested that it might be a good idea to ride on ahead and make dinner arrangements there for the group.

He and another man, George Reid, set off at a canter, the anticipation of a proper dinner strong on their palates. The hills were lightly forested with poplar trees, and unlike the flats, the view forward was limited. Two miles passed, four, then six, with no sign of St. Joseph. All the men could do was continue on. The westering sun reached the horizon and was soon gone in a glorious display of colours. Dusk faded just as quickly into a moonlit night. It was now 10:30 and Sellar had no clear idea where they were except that they had to be north of their starting point. They reined in their horses.

"What do you think, George?" Sellar asked. "Do you think we ought to turn back?"

"Turn back? And say we couldn't find a place as big as St. Joseph? Not on your life!"

Reid dug his heels into his horse's flanks as if to emphasize the point. Sellar followed. Reid was right. If they turned back, what would the guide and the others say of their inability to find St. Joseph? Or more plainly put, of their getting lost? Sellar could almost hear the laughter and the jibes, and he would rather have died than face such an embarrassment. They continued on.

All of a sudden there was the sound of wolves, yapping and howling in the distance — a pack of them, perhaps several packs, the noise was so pervasive. It soon became a terrifying racket that spooked the horses and frightened the men. Foolishly, they had left their guns back in one of the carts and the only weapon they had between them was a belief that Providence was on their side. They carried on, over the rise, while the sound of the wolves seemed to get louder with every step. Then they saw lights in the distance, dim as the first stars at dusk. Relief washed over them, but coming down to the flat, they were stopped by a river. It was the Pembina, and on the far side, they could make out the lanterns and candles glowing in the windows of St. Joseph. The wolves, they would soon discover, were nothing more than the town's 200 sled dogs, kept for winter travel, howling to each other and at the moon.

It was now midnight. "We'd better hold up here," Sellar said, so the men pitched their tent. Since they didn't know where they had even been for the last few hours, let alone where they had left the carts, Sellar knew that their chances of finding the others were slim. He could only hope they hadn't run into a peck of trouble that would cost them all dearly, that the men and animals would arrive safely — and soon. Then two rifle shots came echoing across the night. Sellar was certain that it was the rest of the party seeking direction, but had no gun to answer back. Instead, he rode into the hills toward the noise, found the party and put them on the right trail. At two in the morning, with the dogs finally shut up and peace restored to the prairie, the yowling began all over again as the carts trundled into camp at last, the men and animals more tired than they looked. They had been delayed by an ox that had stampeded when it heard or smelled something it didn't like. The cart was turned over and its contents spilled, while the animal ran off into the night. As if that weren't enough, the cart's axle was broken. And though he was reluctant to admit it, the guide finally confessed that he had also been lost.

Sellar was just glad they had all made it there safe and sound. For him, the worst news was that they would now have to go back in the morning to fetch and repair the cart. It meant more time wasted. Nevertheless, it had to be done, so he and the guide were away at first light and had rejoined their companions back at the Pembina by nine. Together, they forded the river.

St. Joseph was a dismal collection of timber huts with thatched roofs, the poorest of oases in this prairie desert. Sellar supposed that all the residents had to be incorrigibly lazy because none of the land in or out of the village was cultivated, not even for subsistence farming. Beyond the village, the trail was rough but more defined, so that even the guide had no trouble following it. They saw several hundred horses feeding on the rich grass and Sellar presumed they were mustangs. The guide shook his head. "These animals belong to the Métis. They're being strengthened up for the first buffalo hunt of the year in June. Then they'll be back out here by late July or early August getting ready for the next big hunt in September."

They passed through the Fort Pembina area and had no troubles with the Indians gathered there. Upon reaching the Morris River, just where it joined the Red, they swam the cattle across and hired a farmer with a canoe to get everything else over.[5] He charged them 50¢ a cart, which Sellar considered dear but well worth the price, considering it was the last obstacle in their path. The farmer also had a building that passed for a tavern, and those so inclined enjoyed a drink before moving on. Forty miles further on they reached Fort Garry, surprised to discover that the *International* had beaten them by only three days.

"Well done!" McMicking said, impressed with Sellar's story; indeed, impressed with the young man himself. He seemed fearless and resolute, driven more by instinct than by anything else, and would be a good man to have along on the trail. But like a horse given its head, he would probably need to be reined in from time to time.

Since he had arrived in the settlement McMicking had begun gathering all the reliable intelligence about the route to Fort Edmonton that he could lay his hands on. Governor Dallas provided valuable information about what they could expect from the other forts along the route.

"I've sent a courier out to let the factors know that you'll be coming," Dallas said. "I have asked that you be advised of the areas in which you might be vulnerable to Indian attacks. I've also requested that boats be made available to you at all major river crossings. That's as much as I can do. Now I suggest that you go to St. Boniface to see Bishop Taché and arrange for a guide. The best are the Métis and the half-breeds, and the bishop knows them all."

A delegation of three men was formed for the task. They ferried to the east bank and visited the bishop at the cathedral being constructed there. The first man he sent them to was Jemmy Jock Bird, a guide renowned in the colony, but Bird complained of being too old for the job.[6] On the bishop's recommendation they next sought out a man named Charles Racette. A burly, bearded man in his thirties, Racette claimed he knew the route well. He'd been a drover on the Fort Carlton Trail and had done some guiding out of Fort Edmonton. He would take them that far, a distance of 900 miles, and wanted $100 for his trouble. He would expect half of the fee when they got there, while the other half was to be given to Bishop Taché for safekeeping, and handed over to Racette when he returned to the settlement with proof that his obligations had been fulfilled. The overlanders agreed, shook hands on it, then caught the ferry back to the west bank, pleased with how well things had gone.

Once the news spread that Charles Racette had been hired as a guide, word came back that he was not reliable, that he had left parties in the lurch before. McMicking convened an emergency meeting, but the bottom line was that there was not a surplus of guides in the settlement. For better or worse, Racette would have to do.

"All we can do," said McMicking, "is put our faith in him and pray it isn't tragically misplaced. But if he has the smell of flowers about him, we would do well to keep an eye out for a funeral."

By the time Sunday rolled around all of the purchases had been made and McMicking, along with the leaders of the other parties, agreed that it would best to leave Red River and get on the trail as quickly as possible. There were far too many temptations around to distract a man and turn him soft, too many opportunities for drinking and cavorting with the attractive country-born and Métis women who, McMicking believed, lacked the moral scruples of the fine women back home.[7] Besides, the more serious of the men were getting restless, believing that the gold could scarcely be expected to wait until the last man arrived in Cariboo. They decided unanimously to move 25 miles to the west, to White Horse Plain, where there was good pasturage for the many animals they had accumulated, and make final preparations there. They would leave tomorrow, Monday, June 2.

"We've done all we can do," McMicking told the others. "It's now time to act."

Church services had been arranged for the departing gold seekers in the fort's courthouse. During the afternoon the Reverend Griffith Owen Corbett, the Anglican minister, sermonized, and in the evening his Presbyterian counterpart, the Reverend John Black, followed suit. Corbett's service was not inspiring enough to keep all of the men in the hot, stifling room and some left before he finished.[8] Black, on the other hand, demanded his congregation's full attention and got it. He was a lively, indefatigable orator whose theme was identical to Corbett's, that real gold was to be found not in the creeks of Cariboo, but rather in the discovery of God and the Kingdom of Heaven. Most of the men were predisposed to believe this; nevertheless they wouldn't have objected to having a poke or two of the yellow stuff to ease the burden along the earthly path to Heaven's door.

After Corbett's service, cries for help were heard from the river. Someone was drowning and McMicking feared it was a Queenston man. He and Sellar rushed with others to the water's edge. Several men had plunged in to try to save the drowning man but they were too late. Everyone watched aghast as a frantic hand waved above the muddy water, then slipped below the surface. The next day the body of a young man, an employee at the fort, was found caught up on a snag downstream. It caused McMicking to reflect upon Reverend Black's sermon and why the pathway to the Kingdom was so much shorter for some than it was for others. It also reminded him of the dream of drowning he'd had back on Lake Michigan, that he'd all but forgotten.

Sundown came late to this land in summer with only 20 days left to the solstice. The palette of breathtaking colours on the western horizon eventually gave way to the grey-blue of dusk, which in turn surrendered to the night. Isolated pinpoints of light across the sky were slowly joined by an infinity of others to become a gallery of flickering stars and gleaming planets. The wind, more at home here on this prairie than any place on the planet, faded away to a rare stillness. It matched perfectly the mood in the overlander's camp. Most of the men had gone to bed early, the journey ahead and loved ones foremost on their minds. There were silent prayers that all would go well, that Providence would watch over them down the long and difficult road that would begin on the morrow.

McMicking was as excited as he'd ever been in his life. His destiny lay somewhere out there in the west, of that he was certain. He just hoped he was up to the physical challenges of finding it.

Sellar, on the other hand, had no such reservations. He had already completed nearly 500 miles of overland travel, walking at least half of it, and felt fit and ready for the trail ahead. He, like most of the men, was confident they would reach Cariboo some time in August, 60 or 70 days from now, provided they could avoid major problems along the way. That was an average of 25 miles a day, a figure no one seemed to think unrealistic, even allowing for Sunday as a day of rest. There was no denying that it would require a lot of hard work and more than a little luck to pull it off, but if anyone could do it, Sellar was certain that he was the man.

The sky shimmered with stars. The murmur of voices that filled the camp was slowly stilled in the deep blackness of night. From one tent a coughing fit shattered the silence, from another a brief burst of laughter. Somewhere in the dark an arm slipped over the shoulder of a friend, seeking the comfort found in intimacy. A stifled moan here, a sigh there, until the sounds of men gave way to a chorus of frogs singing from the river.

Across the turbid Red the Schuberts were bedded down for the night. The children had been restless earlier on, feeding off the excitement emanating from their parents, and were hard-pressed to find sleep. So were Catherine and Augustus. It had been a busy week and an even busier day, and now they were ready to put this settlement behind them. Catherine felt Augustus slacken into sleep, and when he began to snore softly she found it comforting. She reflected on Fort Garry. What a pity that it hadn't turned out to be what they wanted, that the only hope it offered was the leaving of it. Tomorrow they would be among the gold seekers bound for Cariboo, and this place would be but a memory. Tomorrow they would be gone west. West! Her heart raced with the thought. She lay awake long into the night, and when the children aroused her in the morning, it seemed as if she'd only just dozed off.

Monday morning dawned clear. The sun, already strong in the eastern sky, was sending a message of its intentions for later in the day. The men were up and breakfasting on bacon and beans, and a few even had the luxury of eggs, having gone to the trouble of acquiring some from nearby farms. Afterwards, animals and carts were located, connected and loaded, some with up to 800 pounds of goods. That took most of the morning and after lunch the small city of tents and tarps vanished, transformed into single rolls tied tightly with rope, and secured on top of everything else for easy access. Most of the carts had curved canvas covers, which made them look from a distance like the four-wheel Conestoga wagons used by American pioneers. By five o'clock in the afternoon, they were lined up and ready to move out.

Governor Dallas was on hand to bid them farewell, and offered a final warning about the Indians. "It's not an attack you need fear," he said, "so much as it is theft. They'll steal your horses and anything else they can get their hands on if you are not vigilant!"

Yet many of the men were convinced that thievery was the least of their worries. They envisioned hordes of cannibalistic red men descending upon them, turning the prairie into a sea of blood before devouring their very flesh.

Bishop Taché had come from across the river to bless the expedition and to ask St. Christopher to attend to the overlanders' safety on the way to their destination and beyond. Then the cart train began to move and the settlement erupted in noise. People cheered from the sidelines and cries of "Good luck" and "God bless" were mixed with the sounds of horses whinnying, oxen bellowing and dogs barking. Drivers exhorted animals, and carts squealed and moaned as if to protest that they were designed for something other than movement. All this was set against a background of thudding hooves on prairie earth, patterns in a tapestry of sound. As the column moved out, children and dogs gamboled alongside, unable to contain their excitement. A dust cloud rose and spread, and was carried away to the river by the prevailing breeze. The men, some walking, some riding, were in high spirits, exhilarated, their faces split wide with grins, proud to be part of this great adventure, enjoying being the centre of attention. Soon they had passed the walls of the fort and the last of its satellite buildings, the children and dogs had reached their territorial limits, and the open prairie took them to its breast.

What must it be like, McMicking wondered, to stand at the side of the road and watch as this train of carts, animals and human beings plunged into the unknown? Do they think us mad, or at the very least foolhardy to so willingly partake in an expedition of such a perilous nature? Or do they envy us? He couldn't help but feel a certain amount of pride that he would be among the first to open up communications overland with the goldfields of a far-flung place called Cariboo. That was something to envy, all right.

The cart train followed the Assiniboine River as it twined toward them from the west between tall stands of elm and poplar trees. Once the fort was lost from view a different emotion filled McMicking. Civilization had now been left behind, and other than a small number of forts dotting the plains and the mountain valleys, the next civilized place of stature was 1,500 miles away in Victoria, on Vancouver's Island. Now, every footstep and turn of a cart wheel would lead them deeper into a wilderness that was nothing more than a lot of vagueness on their maps. Looking around he could see an eye or two rimmed with tears, and knew that more than just a few hearts were filled with trepidation. Wasn't his?

Something else bothered him. He hadn't failed to notice the democrat wagon that had joined the end of the train, occupied by two men and accompanied by a man and a woman on horseback. The woman had two baskets slung over her horse with a small child in each, and the man had an older child on the saddle in front of him. Surely they weren't intending on going all the way to Cariboo! This would be no trip for a woman, never mind the children. Obviously they must be on their way to the fort at Portage La Prairie, some 50 miles to the west, and were tagging along with the train for companionship.

Catherine felt anxious and didn't like it at all. Since such feelings were usually alien to her nature, she put it down to being pregnant. That surely had to be the reason. Yet, despite her anxiety, she was pleased that the children seemed content in their baskets, and Gus Jr. looked as proud as only a boy embarking on an adventure with his father could be. She made an effort to smile at Augustus so that he would not worry about her, then fixed her eyes on the long row of carts in front of them.

The train passed several farms growing oats, barley and wheat, but the crops appeared retarded to the easterners, compared to what they were used to. Some of the houses were quite splendid though, one in particular that belonged to James McKay, the renowned Métis guide.[9] Sellar was reminded of his home in the long valley of the Chateauguay River where he had spent a delightfully happy childhood. His heart swelled with emotion, a home-sickness stronger than anything he'd ever felt before. Uncomfortable with such emotions, he chastised himself. They belonged to women and old men, not to a young man in the prime of life. Especially one with a gilded future staring him full in the face.

They reached Sturgeon Creek by eight o'clock and stopped for the night at a good campsite. There was plenty of feed for the animals, which were staked out on short ropes so that they wouldn't wander off. The train was still among scattered farmhouses, and Fort Garry was just seven miles behind, yet it might as well have been 700, so completely removed was the fort from the overlanders' minds.

In the morning everyone was awake early, eager to begin their first full day on the road. Several horses, improperly tethered, had wandered off during the night and a search was undertaken for them. It wasn't a bothersome delay since they wanted to wait for Racette, who had said that he'd catch up with them. By the time the horses were rounded up it was nine o'clock, and the guide had yet to show his face. A poll was taken, and almost everyone deemed it best to move to a supposedly better pasturage at White Horse Plain and wait there. A few chose to stay.

The day soon turned into a comedy of errors as the men learned how to handle their oxen. While a switch across the rump set some in proper motion, it sent others running off with the carts, which turned over and left a trail of supplies through the tall grass. Some even succeeded in shedding their harnesses entirely and escaped in a panic, dewlaps flapping, rearing and bellowing, as if they had completely lost whatever sensibilities they were endowed with. Then they brazenly defied their owners to try and catch them. Some men made lassos and were finally able to capture the animals, but not before one man was jerked off his feet and dragged through the grass for several yards because he refused to let go of the rope. Several others pounced on the rope and eventually restrained the animal.

McMicking, whose own oxen had joined the would-be escapees, viewed the proceedings with fascination and some amusement. My God, he thought, we know nothing about this sort of thing, nothing about the wilderness we are entering. We are clerks and shoemakers, carpenters and bookkeepers, as green as this prairie grass, and I might be the greenest of them all! If we are ever going to make it to the goldfields, Providence had best not leave us to our own devices too often.

Progress was slow, agonizingly so at times, and it was early evening before they reached a small trading post at Pigeon Lake on White Horse Plain.[10] All around them they could see the flat line of the horizon, interrupted only by the tree-lined Assiniboine River, now far to the south. This was a dimension of land and sky that McMicking had never seen before, so vast and so utterly unadorned that he could easily believe this was how the world began and everything else was added to it.

He found beauty in its geometry: a simple horizontal line where the land met the sky, and nothing more. No curves, no complementary angles, no complexities — just a solitary line that had no end no matter which direction he looked. And oh, the colours above those lines at sunrise and sunset! Oranges, reds and purples, occasionally cut by a black line of clouds, and more but he did not have the vocabulary to describe them. Indeed, he wondered if many of the subtle shades even had names. Then the night sky! As many stars could be seen by looking straight ahead as by looking up. It was a dazzling sight. But it was the wind that owned the land. It blew day after day, ceaselessly, sometimes hard, sometimes gentle, but always there, sending shape-changing clouds racing across the sky and their dark shadows dashing over the land; rippling the lush grass in a symbiosis of earth and element and sending shimmering waves of green scurrying toward the horizon. McMicking was reborn. Instead of rendering him insignificant, the boundless land filled and enlarged him. Still, he wasn't so naïve that he didn't know he was seeing the land at its finest, without the plagues of grasshoppers thick enough to stop a train, mosquitoes that would soon be in swarms large enough to kill a horse, drowning floods that turned rivers into lakes, dust storms that eclipsed the daylight and prairie fires that spread so fast they could turn a fleeing man into ashes.[11]

Tents were pitched, firewood was gathered and water drawn. Later, Sellar and several others jumped into the river with soap and had their first real bath of the season. By that time the sun was well down in the sky, shadows were long, and there was a hint of the ghostly legend that gave this place its name, of a white horse that long ago belonged to an Indian girl who was killed by the arrows of a jealous suitor. Before he could capture the horse it escaped into the plains to embody the spirit of the girl and eventually become a ghost.

"We'll not wait around for anyone," Sellar said emphatically the following morning when McMicking suggested that they all wait for a few stragglers who hadn't yet shown up. The Huntingdon party had been first up, and was already breaking camp, Sellar putting the harness on an ox. "There's a long road in front of us that won't be covered sitting on our backsides."

McMicking could not have agreed more, but as one of those most keen to have all the parties travel together, he felt obliged to wait. "But did we not agree to face that road together?"

"Aye, but I'll not be inconvenienced by incompetence."

"I should think it's more inexperience than incompetence. Given a little time they will adjust to their circumstances just as you did. Surely we can wait. There is virtue in it."

"Perhaps so," said Sellar, buckling the harness, "but there is none to be found in idleness." With that, he and the other Huntingdon men finished their preparations and within the half hour they were dust clouds up the road.

McMicking felt rebuffed and it ruffled him. He also didn't like the fact that Racette, who had shown up last night, had left with the Huntingdon party. When he indicated to the guide that his duties lay with the main body of travellers, not the fastest, Racette said that only generals led from the rear. He would lead from the front. Now, watching them disappear up the trail, McMicking hoped that the small confrontation he'd had with Sellar hadn't driven a wedge into their relationship. He was certainly an impatient man, but he was also the most fit, and McMicking was still satisfied that he'd be a good man to have around when the road turned rough, as it most surely would.

Where *were* the others, anyway?

The stragglers arrived after lunch, having had so many problems with their animals back at Sturgeon Creek that they were forced to stay another night. But they seemed to have taken charge of them now, and by three in the afternoon the entire company was on the road. When someone asked if they should fill up their water casks and canteens before leaving, McMicking told them not to bother. Racette had said there was fresh water just three miles ahead, and he ought to know. McMicking felt pent-up and glad to be moving at last, although the stopover had provided an opportunity to meet the Schubert family, who had at least been able to keep up, and find out a little about them.

Schubert himself was tall, angular and gawky, with a straggly beard that appeared to fly off in every direction. He was a man of few words, it seemed to McMicking, and lacked humour, but that was probably because he was Prussian. He had come to America in 1845, when he was just 19, and settled in Massachusetts. By the time he met Catherine ten years later, he had become a carpenter. He seemed a determined man, with a need to get things done, and would be quick to anger if barriers were placed in his way. It was clear that he cared about his children and his wife, and that was important to McMicking.

Mrs. Schubert, though plain, radiated warmth, and her eyes always seemed to be delighted by a joke. Her long dark hair was braided and twirled into a bun. She was Irish, born in Rathfriland, a small village in the shadow of the Mourne Mountains in County Down. Her early teen years were the years of Ireland's "Great Hunger," when famine and typhus had ravaged the country, and villages and fields were haunted by hollow-eyed, skeletal people and an awful stench of unburied, mouldering corpses.[12] Her family was among the lucky ones to escape this nightmare. In 1850, when she was 16, they packed up and left, and were even luckier to survive the ocean voyage to America, a country bold enough to offer them a future. They also settled in Massachusetts.

Catherine was employed as a domestic servant when she met Augustus in 1855, after he had come to her place of employment to do some repair work. He remembered that she had answered the door in a starched white apron over a grey dress, as sure of herself as if she were the mistress of the house. He saw the good humour in her eyes, and enough warmth in her face to make him feel as if he was being welcomed home. A year later they were married, her a Catholic and him a Protestant. She would not have believed such a union possible in Ireland. Within a few weeks of the ceremony, they were on their way west to the Minnesota Territory. They wanted a fresh start, and all the newspapers said that the West was where they would find one.

Seemingly unhindered by being both Irish and Catholic, Mrs. Schubert was altogether quite a fine woman. She smiled easily and was not given to complaining, although it was clear that she was quite willing to share most things on her mind. The children made McMicking miss his own. He was surprised to hear that the family intended to go all the way to the goldfields, for he still didn't think that the trail ahead was any place for women and children. But he kept that opinion to himself for the time being and, not knowing what else to say to them, said nothing. After they introduced him to their two farmhands, André and Pierre, who were driving the democrat, he left.

The late afternoon sun burned hot in a cloudless sky. Seven or eight miles along the trail the overlanders had yet to pass any fresh water, only small alkaline lakes and even smaller, stagnant sloughs. They had long since used up the little water they had, and everyone was thirsty. So were the animals which were beginning to froth at the mouth. The wind had blown away and the land radiated heat like bread fresh from the oven. McMicking was concerned, and called a meeting. Should they go back to Pigeon Lake, where they knew with absolute certainty there was drinking water? Or should they press on and hope that there was some in the offing? A show of hands indicated that no one wanted to turn back. There had to be water somewhere. After all, the

Huntingdon party had obviously not turned back or they would have run into them.

Before long the westering sun dipped below the horizon, turning the sky to scarlet, to rose, to lead grey, until night engulfed the cart train completely. The overlanders might just as well have been stone blind for all they could see, and they had little choice but to give the oxen their heads and hope the animals had the sense to follow the established trail. Several of the men expressed concern that this was probably as good a way as any to get lost, but offered no practical alternatives. Midnight came and they called a halt. The men's thirst was nearly intolerable, but it was the animals doing the heavy work that caused the most concern. What to do now? Everyone was tired enough to stop for the night, but no one wanted to bed down thirsty. They carried on, in hopes of finding water.

The starry night was filled with the din of complaining animals and groaning cart wheels. The air was devoid of moisture, as dry as the choking dust that clogged noses and turned mouths into sandboxes. They trudged on in the darkness, dehydrated and tired. The Schubert children slept in their baskets, and Gus Jr. slept on the horse, leaning into his father's torso. It was nearly two in the morning when those walking noticed that they had to move a little faster to keep up with the carts. The air suddenly felt charged. The oxen were straining forward with more energy than they had shown for some time, and the horses were fidgety. Then the words "water ahead!" rolled back over the train, in stages, until those in the rear had heard the good news.

They had reached Long Lake. Hardly long, and hardly a lake, but it was at least water, and the bullfrogs croaking in the reeds were the most welcome a sound they had heard in a long time. Sellar and the Huntingdon party were there, having also made the trip without water. "You'll need to boil and strain it," he told them, "and it'll still taste like mud, but right about now I don't expect you're too fussy."

He was right. It did the job, and those first few drops were as tasty as sarsaparilla. Then several of the men broke into their rum and whiskey kegs and attended to another thirst that begged slaking.

Questions arose about Racette's competence. Why did he say there would be water where there was none? Shouldn't he have known?

"There's usually plenty of water along that part of the trail." the guide explained, "but I guess it's been a drier year than I thought." Then, as if to justify his oversight, he added, "It's an unpredictable land that you're about to cross, gentlemen, and you would do well to remember that."

The answer appeased some, but many were of the opinion that he should have guessed as much and taken the precautionary measure of having everyone fill their water casks at Pigeon Lake.

Before retiring for the night, an understanding was reached that a general meeting of all parties would be held in the morning. If they expected this journey to be successful, they had to tighten the loose organization that had been formed back in Fort Garry. They needed a leader and, most of all, they needed rules.

After breakfast, 136 people assembled for the meeting. McMicking chaired it. He was already recognized for being well-spoken and intelligent, and there was a timbre to his voice that made people listen. He sat on a water cask while Sellar sat on the ground and took minutes. Over the course of the morning, they reached agreement on the following points that would become their constitution:

First; that this body of men do organize themselves into one body.

Second; that Mr. McMicking be the Captain of this Organization.

Third; that there be a committee formed of all the Captains of the different Companies.

Fourth; that this organization shall be governed by the Captain and guide assisted by the committee.

Fifth; that it shall be the duty of the committee to meet every day at noon and night and arrange the distance to travel and the time to start.

Sixth; that the committee shall draw out a form for watch at night, so that every man shall have an equal proportion to do.

Seventh; that every man pay the sum of one dollar to defray the expense of the guide.

Eighth; that every man comply with the rules, or be subject to such penalty as the captain and committee shall see fit to impose.

Ninth; that there shall be no trading carried on with the Indians, should we meet with any parties on our way, for fear of disputes arising and getting into trouble.

Tenth; that any person who may offend an Indian or Indians, (and in case that his person be demanded in satisfaction) he shall be handed over to their discretion, the Committee to be invested with power to withhold him if they see fit.

Eleventh; that the whole company shall start every morning at 5 A.M. except [if] the Committee see fit to change the hour.

Twelfth; that each company shall take their turn at the head of the train, so that one will have no advantage over the other by always being first and getting the best camping ground and the best supply of wood, etc.

Thirteenth; that there shall be no liquor used amongst the Indians.

Fourteenth; that the whole company be divided into battalions of 21 in number and that three shall watch every night out of each battalion as follows: One from 10 P.M. until 12 midnight; one from 12 until 2:30 A.M., and one from 2:30 until 5:00 A.M.[13]

Other rules were suggested, but these were the ones adopted. As a general order of principle it was also decided that if a cart broke down, the owner had to pull it off to the side of the trail and let those behind him pass. If repairs were effected before the end of the train reached him, he should wait and join the end of it so as not to upset the order. Furthermore, since from this point forward there was a good chance of meeting up with Indians, a plan was adopted for setting up camp at night to prevent animals from being stolen. The carts would be arranged in a triangle with shafts facing outward so as to form a corral, inside which the animals would be kept. The men would pitch their tents on the outside in front of their carts. Six men would be on watch at a time, two on each side of the triangle. Finally, they decided that Sundays would be observed as a day of rest from the trail unless conditions indicated otherwise.

Alexander Fortune, of the Huntingdon party, and one of the new committee members, spoke out on early starts. "No cart or ox should move until the balance of the company is ready to go," he said. "If any man starts before orders from the captain are given then his oxen will be shot."

There were no dissenters.

Of the suggestions that didn't make it into bylaws, one was controversial and was raised because of Catherine Schubert's presence. A motion was put forward that no women be allowed to join the company. There was complete silence for a split second, then everyone started talking at once. McMicking called for order. When the voices settled to a murmur, the Schuberts stepped forward. Augustus held off lighting his pipe so that he could address the chair before Catherine. He could see that her back was up.

"I don't doubt that your intentions are honourable, but they are also misguided. Surely you can use the skills of a good carpenter, which I can offer, and as for Mrs. Schubert, you'll not find a harder worker or greater spirit anywhere. And she knows a remedy or two that could get a man back on his feet again if a fever knocked him flat. If you have concerns for the children, you needn't. They are firmly in our care. And I would think that some of you who've left families behind might find their presence a great comfort."

"There are too many unknown factors," someone spoke out. "Your wife would do well to tend to her hearth and home and leave this road to those more fit to handle it."

Catherine had listened long enough. "Our 'hearth and home' are in that democrat wagon yonder," she said. "Sure, it's a fine man who has the welfare of women and children in his heart, but we've travelled more miles overland than most of you here. And we'd not the luxury of a fancy boat to take us from St. Paul to Fort Garry, nor had we a company of this size to back us up when we stood face to face with Indians along the way."

"Maybe so, but you didn't have to cross any mountain ranges to get here. You will, though, to get to Cariboo, and by all accounts they might serve up more hardship than a woman can endure."

"Well then, you might like to tell the folks here exactly who it was that went over the Oregon Trail in dresses and bonnets. If it was men, then the history books have much to answer for. But I'd wager it was real womenfolk, and that you would've been hard-pressed to find a man in those wagons who wasn't grateful to have 'em along!" She turned and addressed McMicking directly. "Decide what you will, sir, it makes no odds. Whichever way you have it, there'll be a woman on this trail to the goldfields!"

There was muttering from the crowd, and McMicking himself was beginning to have reservations. He liked this woman's grit, and if the smiles on some of the faces in the crowd were any indication, so did many of the other men. They definitely could use her husband's skills, and hers, but there might also be other advantages to having a woman along, particularly one with a family. Any Indians they encountered might be more likely to perceive the group as non-threatening, and a woman's presence would force the men to be on their best behaviour. It was his belief that wherever the fairer sex went, civilization was rarely far behind. He spoke in support of a motion to include women, or at least one woman, and it was carried by a majority. The Schuberts were in.

It seemed to Catherine that McMicking was a fair man, smart, with great integrity and humility. He was a God-loving man, too, and that was good but she wondered what he might think if he knew of the child just beginning to stir inside her. Indeed, they might all be singing a different tune.

By the time the meeting broke up the sun was directly overhead and burning down with a serious intensity, shirts were sticking to sweaty backs, and handkerchiefs were being swiped across sopping brows. The company broke camp, and carts and animals were prepared for the trail. By two o'clock they were under way, McMicking and the Queenston men in the lead of a line of 97 carts that stretched out for nearly a mile across the otherwise empty plain. Long Lake vanished beneath the horizon, and not even the oppressive afternoon heat could stifle the feeling of good cheer and optimism that rose from the train like the clouds of dust from beneath the animals' feet and ever-turning wheels.

On Friday, June 6, the overlanders reached the HBC post at Portage la Prairie, the old portage site for Indians and early explorers travelling between Lake Manitoba and the Assiniboine River. After an uneventful afternoon's drive they camped at a small lake. There were oak stands here, the last to be had on the trail, so the men laid in a stock of wood for repairs to the carts. It was the second night that the carts had been set in a triangle and everyone seemed to think that the system worked well.

Their sixth day on the trail was marked by dramatic changes. The well-travelled cart road between Fort Garry and Portage la Prairie was now only a trail, and the river had swung so far south of their route that its border of trees could no longer be seen. Up until this point the terrain had been flat and uninteresting, but now there was a gain in elevation as the land ever so gradually ascended from what used to be the bottom of Lake Agassiz to its ancient shoreline. Here and there were patches of heavy forest and clear running streams, although some had dried up because the region had been without rain for weeks. A few had treacherous banks and the carts had to be let down by ropes to stop them from overturning. They crossed a large burnt-out area, and saw the devastation of a prairie fire. In contrast to this, considering the drought-like conditions, there were numerous sloughs in which the carts sank to their axles in mud. The men waded into the mire, put their shoulders to the wheels and pushed. At first they removed their socks and shoes and rolled up their pants, but after a while they realized that it was only wasting time and plunged in fully dressed. The cool mud helped little in preventing salty rivulets of sweat from rolling down their burnished faces, stinging their eyes when they weren't able to wipe it away. And the insects in those damp places were maddening.

"Let's spread the carts out as much as possible," Racette told the company. "It'll be a lot easier getting through these areas if we're not following in each other's wake."

It was good advice. The men also learned that while the oxen could easily pull an 800-pound load on the flat, it was a different story over rough or muddy terrain. Loads were redistributed so that the heaviest was around 600 pounds. And as the miles wore on, they realized that the daily travel routine they had set up wasn't working. So far, the camp had been aroused at four A.M., and one hour was allowed for breakfast and to make the carts ready. Then they drove till eleven A.M. before stopping for lunch and to let the animals feed. Back on the trail again by two P.M., they drove through till six P.M. This gave them ten solid hours of travelling. However, it became clear that the animals were not happy with the six-hour drive in the morning. It was far too long to go without food and water and the beasts suffered for it, so the schedule was changed. The company awakened at two-thirty A.M. to start at three A.M., without breakfast. They drove for two hours, then stopped for two hours to feed themselves and the animals. Under way again by seven A.M., they drove four more hours before stopping two hours for lunch, after which they drove till six P.M. This was not only easier on the animals, it gave them an extra hour of travel.

They supplemented their food supplies with ducks, usually stuffed with wild onions and leftover bread, and even scoured the marshes daily for duck eggs. This diet was rounded out with wild turnips and a wide variety of berries. The men who had come from cities and towns in the east were astonished at how bountiful the land was.

They were pleased with their progress, thus far. They had managed to put a hundred miles between themselves and Fort Garry, and what's more, they were much improved for it. Every mile that had passed was another mile of experience, and the men were becoming proficient at handling the animals and carts. For many, the aching, stiff muscles of the first two or three days were gone, and they were feeling fit. One hundred miles. No small feat for men who, less than two months before, were clerks, cabinet makers, teachers and a host of other occupations that kept them inside and physically inactive. Still, it was a staggering concept, even for the staunchest of them, that there were more than a thousand miles yet to go. Nevertheless, 20 miles one day, 30 another, eventually added up to a destination. The trick was to turn the days into separate parcels of time and energy. Plan ahead yes, but focus completely on the task at hand, and before a man knew it he had done what he wanted to do, and was where he wanted to be.

Their first Sabbath on the road passed with the company in fine fettle. Though it was a day of rest from the trail, everyone was kept busy making repairs to the tackle and carts, or taking the opportunity to wash their clothes in the stream, a domestic and menial chore that was a necessary evil for most. A few who could afford it hired Catherine to do it for them, but she could only do so much, what with children and a husband to look after. Nevertheless, it was an opportunity that few others had to earn money, and for that she was grateful. It was her nature to work hard and it was a bonus to be paid for it.

McMicking was one of the fortunate few to avail themselves of Catherine's services, and he admired the good spirit in which she carried out her work. It was little wonder, though, that such labour accounted for the ruination of many a good woman's sweet disposition. It certainly would make him miserable.

At moments like these he envied Augustus not having to do such chores: envied, most of all, that the man had his family with him. He missed Laura and the children terribly, and got a knot in his stomach just thinking about them. But he knew that they would not have fared well in these circumstances. He recalled the glorious summer Sundays they had shared at the beach, and the exciting jaunts up to the Falls to see Blondin and Signor Farini walk tightropes across the Niagara River.[14] What a joy it was to share time together as a family! He was flooded with impatience to have this journey over with, when it had hardly begun. "We are not born to be alone," he recalled Laura saying, one night after they had made love. "Life only has meaning when it is shared intimately with someone." Her words only made him feel worse, so he went off to speak to Racette before he grew hopelessly maudlin.

In the afternoon a religious service was held. Alexander Fortune read from the scriptures. Fortune was a serious man with great passion and exuberance. Below his meticulously combed black hair, his wide face sloped to a narrow chin and he wore thick muttonchops to compensate for it. He was 31, and in his youth had studied for the Presbyterian ministry, but had given it up for health reasons. A humane man, he was more sensitive than most to the plight of the Indians, although it hadn't stopped him from bringing along his best gun and a good stock of ammunition just in case he had to fight them on his way across the plains. Nevertheless, it was his belief that all life should be treated with respect. He saw his ox as truly one of God's creatures and scrupulously tended to its needs. He believed God was everywhere, and in all things. For this day's reading he chose Christ's sermon to the multitudes in Matthew's book, and ended with verse 24 from chapter 6. It wouldn't hurt to remind everyone of the lessons taught by Black and Corbett back in Fort Garry: "No man can serve two masters; for either he will hate the one, and love the other; or else he will hold to the one and despise the other. Ye cannot serve God and mammon."

The service was finished with some hymn singing, voices raised heavenward for God's pleasure, but the refrains were scattered by the winds out over the prairie and swallowed up by the extraordinary silence.

Monday morning found the cart train in two sections: a long one consisting of those who were ready on time, and a short one made up of those who weren't. There was protesting from the latter who were accused by some of malingering, but all McMicking said was, "We've established a time to leave in the mornings, gentlemen, and you need to put every effort forward to meet it. Otherwise, lodge your complaints with the trees. You'll meet with more sympathy from them than you will from the rest of us."

The first part of the trail took them through soft, coarse, yellow sand and, as in mud, the carts were fanned out in several V-shaped formations. The weather remained dry and stifling, and the gadflies and sand fleas tortured both man and animal. By mid-morning the train was crossing Pine Creek, the bed of which was obligingly hard, and the trail began to improve, through lush grass seven to eight feet high.

Early the next morning the Whitemud River was not quite so accommodating. The banks were soft and marshy, and though the river wasn't wide, its bed was unstable. A makeshift bridge had to be built to cross it, and while the trail down to the bridge wasn't too much of a problem, getting up the slippery slope on the far side presented the men with a gruelling start to the day.

"Don't stop!" McMicking shouted, irritated. "Keep them moving!" But someone stopped anyway, near the top, and once stopped the ox could not get moving again. An extra animal had to be hitched up to pull the cart free. Then everyone behind the stopped cart got stuck too, and tempers flared among those delayed by what they perceived to be a clear case of stupidity. The train was a full two hours crossing this innocuous-looking stretch of water, by which time the men were as weary as if they had already put in a full day's work.

Afterward, one man blamed the entire episode on the first man to stop. Angry words flew back and forth and there was a flurry of fists. Others quickly stepped in to break up the fight, but the first blows had already dampened the combatants' ardour. Other than a few minor bruises the men had only their foolishness to deal with. Meanwhile, an ox ran off with its cart and had got a half dozen miles away before it was rounded up.

McMicking was annoyed by the event, and told the men that their behaviour was unacceptable. "A fist thrown at another man shows a lamentable lack of ideas," he said. "If you feel you've run out of them perhaps you might find what you need at a general meeting, or in one of Mr. Fortune's sermons. It's a decidedly more civilized way of doing things."

The air was hot and a line of towering clouds that had been building on the southwestern horizon since lunchtime greeted them late in the afternoon. A sound like cannons rumbled across the sky and in the near distance jagged bolts of lightning streaked to the ground. A cool, almost violent, wind shouldered its way through, but it was the lightning that frightened everyone and they crawled beneath their carts for protection. Catherine and Augustus, along with their wide-eyed children and two farmhands huddled beneath the democrat and awaited the storm's passage there. Despite the cracks of thunder and flashes of lightning, Gus Jr. insisted that he be allowed to play out in the rain, which had begun pelting down so hard on the tarps protecting the supplies in the wagon that it sounded like hail. Then it stopped as suddenly as it had started and the storm rolled on to the northeast. They crawled out of their makeshift shelter, reasonably dry, thankful that they had caught only the storm's edge. It was just enough to cool things down but not enough to turn the trail into a river of mud.

On the following day, after a morning's drive over a rough and swampy trail, they came to the high banks of the Minnedosa River. McMicking found the 200-foot-deep valley stunningly beautiful, as fertile as anything he'd seen. It at first looked formidable, but proved to be otherwise. The river was only 40 feet wide and three to four feet deep at the ford, and in just three-quarters of an hour the entire train had gained the top of the far bank. Pleased with their accomplishment and by the lush scenery, they stopped for lunch, fishing for pike and admiring the myriad swans gracing the river.

For the rest of the day the cart trail wound among small lakes and in places was so rough and boggy that travelling was difficult. In other places the grass was so high they could scarcely see over it. Wild peas were plentiful, and there was an abundance of clover for the animals. The company had now gained about a thousand feet in elevation since leaving Fort Garry.

One of the men had fallen ill, and when Catherine found out, she sent Augustus back a half mile or so to gather some of the white, daisy-like flowers she'd seen growing alongside the trail. At lunchtime she brewed tea from the flowers' petals, and bade the man drink it. "Sure it's good for what's ailing you," she said, "and if it isn't, it'll do you no harm." But he was much improved by morning, and gave Catherine full credit for it.

They came to Shoal Lake, as pretty a place as any they had seen, pristine and crystal clear, and full of fish impatient for a baited hook. It was early, but they set up camp anyway. There was a fry-up of pike that night, the likes of which no one had ever experienced before, and later, after all chores had been attended to, musical instruments were dug out from beneath tarps and out of trunks. There were enough to make up a small orchestra: violins, clarinets, flutes, a variety of brass instruments, a concertina, and the best instrument of all, the human voice. Altogether there were about 30 musicians and even more singers, and it was glorious. McMicking reckoned that they would have sounded like a real orchestra and choir if one ignored the flats and sharps that weren't supposed to be there. Songs like "The Old Oaken Bucket" and "Castles in the Air," swept out over the prairie like the morning sun, and it was the sound of pure joy. They sang a rousing version of "The Yellow Rose of Texas," taught to them by James Wattie of the Huntingdon party, who said he had learned it on the creeks of California. One of the Acton men sang a plaintive, melodic song he had been taught by a half-breed girl in Fort Garry.

O consider a while ere you leave me,
Do not hasten to bid me adieu,
But remember the Red River Valley,
And the half-breed that loved you so true.

The music became so lively that some began to dance, and the trampled grass became their ballroom as men swung around men, bumping into each other and laughing, while others clapped in time with the music to spur them on.

Sellar was in the midst of the revelry, letting it fill him up until it overflowed. He could neither play an instrument, nor sing, but he had two legs that wouldn't keep still and if that wasn't suited to dancing, then nothing was. As far as he was concerned, he might have been in one of the best dance halls the Canadas had to offer. It could have been better only if Mary Jane, his recent bride, were there to share the evening with him, but he took Catherine for a couple of turns around the "dance floor" and by God, didn't that feel good! Even if she was Catholic.

McMicking joined in for a while, then took a stroll along the lakeshore to enjoy some solitude. He lit his pipe and blew out smoke contentedly. The western sky was streaked with a glorious array of colours, another spectacular sunset in a land that seemed to hold the patent on them. The lake was as smooth as marble and mirrored the sky. Clouds of tiny insects hovered over the water near the reeds, and now and then fish rose and broke the surface into outward-spreading rings. What a perfect night, he thought. And oh, the wonder of music! More than anything else in the world it helps us understand that we are not alone with our feelings, that the joy and sorrow we feel is the same joy and sorrow everyone else feels. Music unites us.

Such evenings, he knew, would be conducive to good morale, and for that reason alone he had insisted that they be as much a part of this journey as observing the Sabbath — as long as time and circumstance allowed. He hoped it would be often. He also hoped that the expedition would continue to go well, praise God, and he took a moment to offer a small prayer of thanks. He prayed too that a seed of concern that had been growing in his mind would not bear fruit.

He had noticed a certain aloofness on Racette's part and suspected there were things going on in the man's mind that he was unwilling to communicate. McMicking did not like it when the guide went off with the first cart out in the morning, and as a result was often not available for consultation. And that was another thing. Sellar and Wattie and some of the other Huntingdon men were getting up earlier and leaving before everyone else. They wanted an untrampled trail to travel on and the best campsites at the end of the day, which was contrary to the agreement made back at Long Lake. They were supposed to take turns. He wondered why Fortune, who at least had the good sense to leave with the main body, hadn't said anything about it.

He usually had no trouble voicing his opinions. Perhaps it was because he was a Huntingdon man himself and just wanted to keep the peace. Sooner or later, though, McMicking knew the problem would have to be dealt with. Meanwhile, there was still a long way to go and it would eventually be resolved. He would have to make sure of it.

The music washed through him, and out across the lake. Considering the extent to which sound carried over water, he wouldn't have been surprised if it could be heard clear to the far end — had there been human life there to hear it. Regardless, those musical notes wafting through the wilderness were surely an announcement of civilization's inexorable advance, with all its wonders and all its wrinkles. He and the rest of the company were opening a door through which many others were bound to enter.

Later, when the Schuberts had bedded their children down and were themselves preparing to retire, Catherine reflected upon the past few days. She was glad of the service, of the strength of conviction in Fortune's bible readings, but thought it would be much nicer if there were a priest along to hear confession. And then tonight — Lord, what a party! Her feet felt like they'd been danced down to stubs. And here they were in the back of beyond! She hadn't done that since she was a child in Ireland, at the *siasmas* that filled Irish souls as full as potatoes filled Irish bellies, before both means of sustenance had been stolen from them by famine and fever.[15] It was always so good to be full! As she crawled beneath her covers, she was in need of a bath, but that would have to wait till morning. The tune from one of the songs had been playing over and over in her head. It was a catchy refrain, but all she could remember was the chorus that began: "She's the sweetest rose of colour that Texas ever knew, Her eyes are bright as diamonds, they sparkle like the dew...."

Mr. Wattie had said that the "Yellow Rose" was a mulatto girl, the servant of an officer during the revolution in Texas. She must have been quite a beauty to have inspired such a fine song. Would that we all could be so fortunate as to have songs written for us, Catherine mused. She teetered on the edge of sleep for a time, then fell in.

It had been a good day and an even better night, and the music, stories and laughter went on for some time. But the day's toil eventually caught up with everyone, and the making of music was finally left to the frogs in the reeds, the loons on the lake and the crackling of wood in the campfires kept going by the guards.

On Friday, the overlanders passed through a succession of small hills, valleys, wooded groves and lakes enlivened by a variety of colourful flowers — wild roses, wild peas and many that didn't even have names yet. They forded two more tributaries of the Assiniboine and, a few miles farther on, Birdtail Creek. The creek ran through a ravine nearly 500 feet deep, but the trail descended gradually down a treeless side gully, nearly a mile long, to the waterside. This creek was the first they had crossed to have a rocky bed, rather than silt, and it presented problems of its own. In places the rocks were unstable, which caused the carts to lurch badly, and this in turn put great strain on the axles. But it was only a couple of feet deep and 30 wide so the fording went well. And Providence had kindly placed another gradually sloping side gully on the far bank for an easy climb back to the level prairie.

For Sellar, the beauty of land they were passing through was unsurpassable. It inspired him to poetry. He pulled out his small, leather-bound diary, flipped past the dog-eared pages crammed

full with his nearly indecipherable jottings to the first blank page
and wrote:

> Where the wild rose and peas in abundance
> Does bud and blossom and fade away unseen
> And waste their beauty and fragrance far away
> Upon a lonely western prairie green.[16]

Better to concentrate on poetry, he thought, than to let the
mind fill with horrific images of warring Indians. From here on
out they would have to be doubly watchful, for they were about
to enter a vast arena of conflict. The two factions involved were
the Cree and Blackfeet. As the prairies opened up to commerce
and settlement, the Cree, whose roots were in the eastern plains
and woodlands, had been pushed westward into the central plains,
traditionally the land of the Blackfeet. The tribes had been at
each other's throats for some time now, and it would do no one
any good, least of all the overlanders, to get caught between them.
At best, they might lose their supplies. At worst, their lives. It
might be a good plan to start greasing the axle wheels, Sellar
reasoned, in order to reduce the noise of their passage. He would
mention that to McMicking the first chance he had.

In the morning they drove eight miles over a stony trail, the
carts teetering along the bumpy terrain like tiny boats caught in a
chop. By mid-morning they stood on the high bluffs above the
valley of the Assiniboine River.

The panorama before them was stirring. The valley, cut through
the prairie by the river, was 250 feet deep and more than a mile
wide between opposing bluffs. The sides were wooded and steep,
the reed-edged river broad and deep, the first truly imposing

obstacle in their path thus far. Across the way, on a distant rise, was Fort Ellice, sitting high above Beaver Creek where it sliced through the hills from the west to join the Assiniboine.

The HBC had a scow tethered by a loop that slid over a rawhide rope spanning the river. On this day the vessel happened to be on the far side, so without being asked, Sellar doffed his clothes, dove in, and swam across to retrieve it. A crude affair, it hardly seemed up to the job required of it, but it could handle one ox and cart per crossing and this was deemed preferable to stripping the carts and floating them over.

The others began to unhitch the oxen. Since the sides of the valley were too steep for a proper trail the carts would have to be lowered by rope, one at a time, and the animals led down. It was tedious, heavy work in the oppressive mid-day heat, and the flies and mosquitoes were merciless. The river bank was marshy, making it difficult to gain access to the scow, and it got worse as the men, animals and carts churned it into mud. Using ropes tied to each end of the scow the men pulled it back and forth across the relentless current more than a hundred times. On the far side, a rugged trail, hacked through the thick growth of trees along the side of Beaver Creek, ran at a manageable gradient to the top of the bluff. The oxen were re-hitched and driven up it. The entire day had passed before the last of the company had crossed the river and gained the flat land above, with Fort Ellice just a yell down the trail.

The old post had seen better days; in fact a replacement fort was under construction two miles away, on a bluff above the Qu'Appelle River. Even so, its halcyon days as a fur-trading post were gone, and the new one would be little more than a provisions store for those passing through on the Fort Carlton Trail.

William McKay, the master of the fort, was accommodating and hospitable, while looking out for the Company's interest at the same time. He charged the travellers 50¢ per cart for the use of the scow.[17] "It will also pay for use of the other Company scow on the Qu'Appelle River," he said, "which is capable of hauling two animals and two carts per crossing."

It was still a king's ransom as far as McMicking was concerned, and he hoped that the scow on the Qu'Appelle was in better condition than the one on the Assiniboine, which was more suitable for firewood. But they were at the Company's mercy, were they not?

As the men pitched the tents and prepared camp, a bank of ominous-looking clouds was building in the southeast, a harbinger of inclement weather. At this stage it wasn't much of a concern. Tomorrow was the Sabbath and they were not going anywhere.

They awoke to a cold, inhospitable rain that obscured the prairie. After effecting cart repairs and taking on new provisions from the fort's supplies, as many of the company as could squeeze into McKay's residence gathered for a religious service. There was an ordained minister of the Anglican Church on hand to conduct it, which, for most of the attendees, was welcome news, but few failed to hide their surprise upon discovering that the minister was a full-blooded Cree. He was the Reverend James Settee, one of only two native Anglican ministers. Gregarious and energetic, his broad smile and happy disposition quickly affected everyone. By the time the service was done, he'd won them all over, the skeptics included, and was considered to be well deserving of his exalted office.

Alexander Fortune had been elected to speak to Racette about going off with the first carts in the morning, instead of waiting for the main body and orders from Captain McMicking. He had not been looking forward to it, for he found the man belligerent and unapproachable. Nevertheless, after the service, Fortune pulled the guide aside. "I have been asked to remind you, Racette, that your responsibilities are to this company as a whole, and not to those who arise before everyone else just so they can be first on the road. Your orders come directly from Captain McMicking, and no one else."

The guide seemed uninterested. "I'm aware of where my orders come from, but as I told the captain, generals lead from behind, guides do not. Besides, it is your own men who bribe me with rum and flattery to leave with them."

Fortune hoped Racette was lying. If he wasn't, it meant that the Huntingdon men, particularly Sellar and Wattie, were the culprits. They were always the first to be ready and away. But could the guide be believed?

"We'll see about that," he said. "Meanwhile, you would do well to remember that your pay comes from Captain McMicking and not from the Huntingdon men."

With little sincerity Racette promised that from now on he would listen only to McMicking. Then without waiting for a signal from Fortune that the conversation had ended, he turned his back on him and walked away.

"Racette will listen only to Racette," the guide muttered to himself, "and no one else." He recalled a trip four years earlier, when some Americans had hired him to guide them from Fort Edmonton through the Rockies to the Kootenays, where they would find another guide to take them to the gold bars of the lower Fraser River. They headed south to the Kananaskis River and Sinclair Pass. This was mid-October, and some Indians they met said there were several feet of snow in the mountains. His first glimpse of the Rockies alarmed Racette and he knew that only a fool would try to cross such a barrier at this time of year. But the Americans had dreams of gold clouding their vision and would not turn back. The next morning he pointed to the route that his charges should follow, and said that he was going to hunt some game and would catch up with them. The Americans were suspicious, and Racette could feel their guns pointing at his back as he rode off. But they never fired, and he never returned. He went back to Fort Edmonton with the money the men had paid him in advance, safe in his saddle bag.[18] Racette listens to Racette, and no one else.

Fortune went directly to McMicking and described his conversation with the guide.

"We need to be careful about making accusations," McMicking said, "especially when we only have Racette's word for what's been going on. Nevertheless, the business of early departures needs to be addressed. I will call a general meeting as soon as there's a decent break in the weather."

But the rain continued throughout the rest of the day and the next, hard and slanting, and looked as if it might never quit.

Three days later the company was gathered in a downpour at the edge of the bluff above the Qu'Appelle River. They had stayed over an extra day at the fort, hoping the weather would clear, but other than a couple of brief lulls the rain still hadn't let up. Since they couldn't afford to wait any longer, McMicking had ordered them out. Now they had to get down this steep incline without bringing harm to either man or beast. It wasn't yet slick with mud, but it soon would be. The first few carts and animals would see to that.

After a brief discussion as to the best way to negotiate the slope, McMicking assigned two men to each cart, one to lead the ox and the other, using only his bare hands, to pull back on the spokes of the wheel, as a kind of brake to slow the descent. Over the crest the first team went, slowly, both men digging in their heels to keep the ox and cart at a safe pace. The lead man's feet slipped from under him, but he quickly regained his balance and they reached the river without further incident. Others followed, just as gingerly, but the ground was soon beaten into mud and grew more precarious with each unit descending it.

Bill Morrow, a merchant from Montreal, and Dobson Prest, a carpenter from Queenston, were working together, Morrow leading and Prest working the wheel. They were a quarter of the way down the slope when the ox panicked because it couldn't get purchase in the mud. The animal surged forward and the forceful movement jerked Morrow off his feet and threw him tumbling downhill in front of the cart. Prest tried his best to hold the wheel, but it was too much for him. He let go. Morrow struggled for traction in the greasy mud, but couldn't find a foothold to launch himself clear of the ox and cart hurtling toward him. He managed to avoid the ox but fell in the path of the cart's right wheel. It ran over his head, which disappeared into the muck. The ox and cart went careering wildly down the slope. Horrified, Prest let out a yell and slid down the hill to his companion, who wasn't moving. He pulled him from the mud, fearing the worst. There was more shouting up and down the slope, until word got back to Eady Stevenson, a certified medical doctor. He grabbed his bag and hurried to the accident site. Catherine went along, too, in case she could help.

Morrow was unconscious, but he was breathing. "Let's get his head up-slope," said Stevenson, and they carefully turned him. He was slathered in mud, but someone brought a cloth and between that and the rain they cleaned him. He came to, and other than being slightly bewildered, seemed to have all his faculties. Prest was certain that his friend's head had been crushed. Hadn't he seen the heavy cart wheel run over it with his own eyes? But by some miracle Morrow's skull was intact. The only damage Stevenson could find was to the man's ear, which had been shredded by the wheel.

"It must have been because the mud is so deep," Prest said. "His head didn't meet any resistance when the wheel ran over it — it was just pushed farther into the mud."

It was the only plausible explanation they could come up with.

"Aye," said Catherine. "We used to say in Ireland that a lucky man is one who's been thrown in the sea and comes up with a fish in his mouth. I'd say that Mr. Morrow has come up with a whale."

Stevenson checked for broken bones elsewhere, and found none. He dressed the wound and ordered Morrow to spend the next few days convalescing as a passenger in one of the carts.

McMicking was shaken by the incident. Minor though it may have been, this was their first casualty, and he alone was responsible for it. As the slope got muddier, he should have put more men on each cart, or had them lowered down by rope. It won't happen again, he promised himself. He would err on the side of caution from now on, rather than risk leaving a man's bones to moulder in this empty land.

From the landing on the north bank the company followed the river upstream for two miles. The trail was sandy and made slow going, but at least it wasn't slick with mud. They eventually came to another trail that took them out of the valley and back to the level prairie again. They set up camp at a fresh-water spring, a few miles from the Qu'Appelle. The rain persisted, heavy and drenching.

The tents leaked badly. Water seeped through the hand-sewn seams until it seemed as wet inside as it was outside. Everything was damp, if not soaked, and mildew grew white in folds and in hidden places. There was no way to get dry. They could not light a fire, either for warmth or for cooking. The temperature had dropped fiercely, and they shivered from the cold, there on the verge of the summer solstice. They went to bed in wet clothes, wrapped in sodden blankets. There was nothing else to do.

In the Schubert tent, Augustus and Catherine put the children between them and huddled together for warmth. "Ah, it could be worse," Catherine told them, "we're not drowned yet!"

You had to be Irish and have made an ocean passage on an emigrant ship to know the true meaning of misery, she thought. Six weeks crammed nose to nose, breathing someone else's foul breath, sleeping on rotting timbers amid the stink of human filth, without food enough to stop the rumbling in your belly or water enough to moisten the cracks in your lips — now that was misery! Aye, things could indeed be worse. She placed an arm over her children and when she heard their measured breathing, fell asleep herself.

As for the rest of the camp, most of the men had never been more miserable in their lives. Since most could not sleep, there was ample time to ponder exactly what they were doing in this wilderness, in this rain, in this cold.

Eustache Pattison, a bookish 19-year-old from Toronto, was wide awake, stretched out on his back and staring into the night, pondering harder than most. His tent-mates were silent, finished their grumbling about the rain, and either lost in their own concerns or asleep if they were lucky enough. It was the lure of gold that had brought him here, no doubt about that, but to be honest he had never stopped to think about what might be in store for him between the lure and the gold. From the safety and comfort of his home, it had seemed such an easy thing to do, to cross the country by land, but now he wasn't so sure. Now he just wanted to go home. Had he owned all the gold in the world, he would have traded most of it for the succor of a warm, drying fire. The rest he'd give for a swift passage back to Toronto. He sniffed as quietly as he could, thankful for the blessed darkness hiding the tears that filled the corners of his eyes and occasionally spilled over to roll down the sides of his face.

To everyone's relief, the rain stopped by morning and the sky began to clear, though it was unseasonably cold. The trail in front of them was flat and sandy and they made good time over it. The lunch stop provided a perfect opportunity for McMicking to call the general meeting he'd wanted back at Fort Ellice.

He opened by stating that most of the company were unhappy with the train being fragmented. He did not name names, or parties, since everyone knew who the culprits were. He especially did not mention Racette's accusation. It would serve no good purpose to do so, and he hoped that the guide would remain silent. He simply stated points 11 and 12 of the company's constitution: that everyone would leave at the same hour, and that each party would have an opportunity to lead so that no single party would have the advantage of the best trail, best camp site and best firewood.

It was Wattie who spoke out. "It's difficult sticking to those bylaws when many of the company are so slow."

Sellar cut in, his voice rising, "And that's because there are too many people who don't know a damned thing about oxen and carts! All they seem to be good for is standing around and watching while others do the work for them. They might do all right as a clerk back home, but that kind of experience is no good out here if they're stuck in a mudhole!"

"Right," said Wattie evenly. "We need to do something about the workloads. I think it would be better for all of us if we changed our rules so that everyone had to be involved in the work. It's the only way we'll get this train to run more efficiently. Maybe we can assign specific jobs for setting up and breaking camp, even during lunchtime stops. We could have one group of men tend the animals, while another group draws water for cooking and washing up. Other people could cook, collect firewood, repair and grease carts and so on. In other words, I'm suggesting we adopt a more formal kind of organization that would see us all away on time *and* together."

Wattie's logic was indisputable. McMicking had recognized the need to do something for a while now, not only because some of the rules were being ignored, but because the company's progress thus far was so slipshod. They had been operating more like a collection of individuals than a unit. "Those are sound ideas, Mr. Wattie, and I thank you for them. I would add only that the more we operate with military precision, the better off we'll all be. The more disciplined we are, the better our chances of getting to where we're going, as well as doing it with a minimum of fuss. I think that we ought to implement your suggestions immediately."

A motion was called for, seconded and carried by a majority. The committee of party leaders began drawing up a list of chores and assigning men to do them. The changes had an immediate effect. There was a greater sense of community, and those who had been willing to let others bear the brunt of the workload were all the better for being given direction. It occurred to McMicking that all men want to be productive but some find it impossible without being told what to do.

Such was the newly felt buoyancy of the company that by the end of the day they had covered 30 miles, the best day's travel yet. They set up camp on the west side of Cutarm Creek, and marvelled at how quickly the task was accomplished. There was a good feeling among the men, and no one seemed to be nearly as bothered now by the ants that crawled into everything, and the hellish battalions of mosquitoes that ravaged them.

Everyone was allowed a bit of a sleep-in the next morning as a reward for the previous day's hard run. They arose at 3:30 A.M., planning to be on the trail at four, but the ground was white with frost and there was a thin skin of ice on the water in the kettles. The animals couldn't feed very well on the frosty grass, so McMicking delayed the departure time till 6:30 to give them an opportunity to fill their bellies. As the tents were being struck, he went looking for Racette to discuss the day's plans.

"He's gone off hunting," Eustache Pattison said. "I even loaned him my gun to do it. Said he'd be back by the time we're ready to pull out."

McMicking merely nodded, but there wasn't a thing he liked about what he'd just heard. When seven o'clock came and went, he liked it even less. "We'll go," he told the party captains. "Racette should be along soon."

But he didn't believe it. The reserve he'd noticed in the guide back at Shoal Lake had increased with each passing day, and since Fortune's remonstration, the man had become even more distant, speaking only when he was spoken to, and was often belligerent. When lunchtime rolled around and Racette had still not shown up, he was certain the guide had deserted. Damn the man for the traitor that he was!

Over the course of the afternoon the train passed through a land broken by hummocks and stippled with groves of poplar trees. The sun was pleasantly warm, as if summer had decided to return to the prairies. When camping time arrived and Racette had still not appeared, McMicking convened another meeting.

"I believe it has become apparent to everyone that our guide has deserted," he addressed the crowd. "Thus we now have some important decisions to make."

There were cries of outrage from the company. "He deserves nothing less than hanging!" shouted one, and another yelled, "Hanging's too good for the scoundrel!"

"Hold on a moment!" This from Alexander Robertson, a young surveyor from Goderich. "Racette told me that he'd been threatened by some members of the more ambitious parties who liked to be away fast and first in the morning, that if he didn't ride with them, he would come to physical harm!"

It was a direct assault on the character of the Huntingdon men, and they protested loudly.

McMicking's gavel was a stick, and he banged it on a water cask to gain control of the meeting. "Unless you have solid evidence to support such an accusation, Robertson, it would be best to keep it to yourself. The fact is, Racette has a reputation for deserting, and we knew that when we contracted his services.

A blind man could have seen the changes in his attitude over the last couple of weeks which, in my belief, were consistent with someone who was about to jump ship."

Sellar interrupted, pointing out that in addition to the $50 they had left with Bishop Taché in St. Boniface, they had paid the guide $20 so far. "This means we're out of pocket $70, not counting the food he ate and the gun that he stole. So the man's a bloody thief as well as a traitor! And it wouldn't surprise me in the least to find that he and that damned bishop conspired to bilk us out of our money!"

"Hear! Hear!" This from the more ardent Protestants in the crowd who needed little convincing that any Catholic would be capable of such a crime.

McMicking was appalled by the indictment and quickly came to Taché's defense. "We must consider the sanctity of his office," he insisted, "and acquit him of any possibility of collusion. As far as Racette is concerned, he should be exposed for the villain that he is so that others will know of his crimes. But right now we have to decide what to do. Shall we turn back and give up the hard-earned ground we've won? Or should we carry on and complete the task we set for ourselves back in Fort Garry, indeed, back in our hometowns? I understand that the trail ahead is well marked, and we should have little trouble finding our way. But it is up to you to decide. Shall we give in or keep going?"

A mighty roar of approval rose from the crowd, followed by three cheers for the company and another three for McMicking.

He had his answer.

"We are decided, then," he said, and banged his stick on the water cask as if to seal their fate. "I would add a cautionary note, though. We will have to be even more vigilant now, and double the watches. There's an outside chance that the blackguard will return with some Indians to do us all in!"

McMicking was grateful for the unanimity of the company, for this was no place to start disintegrating. Yet despite his denunciation of Racette, he was left with an uneasy feeling. Was it possible that the guide had indeed been pulled in a variety of directions by members of the different parties and simply got fed up with it? If that was the case, then they had no one but themselves to blame for their predicament.

So the company moved on, guideless. Scouts were sent ahead on horseback to ensure that they were following the right trail, which presumably was one that looked the most travelled. Each mile they put behind them only served to build their confidence, as various landmarks confirmed the intelligence given them by Mr. McKay at Fort Ellice. They crossed a wide, open, treeless plain dotted with small alkaline lakes and completely devoid of drinking water. Indeed, the water wasn't fit even to wash their clothes — the alkali turned the soap into glue that was almost impossible to wash out — and one of the lakes smelled so strongly of sulfur it nearly suffocated them. Strangely enough, though, there were more ducks on these lakes than they had ever seen concentrated in one place.

There were sloughs near some of the lakes that might have posed a problem, but plenty of brush grew around them to cut and use as fill to cross them without getting stuck. To add to their anxiety about the plans Racette might have for them, they spotted a small band of Indians, two on horseback and the rest on foot. Word of their presence spread to the rear of the train like wildfire. There were some tense moments as the men checked their weapons, but the Indians made no effort to approach the train and disappeared in the distance. The watches that night were doubly alert, and the more fertile imaginations among the overlanders had little trouble conjuring up an image of the band returning with thousands of other Indians and slaughtering the lot of them while they slept.

As each day wore on, clothes and boots wore out, blisters ballooned and burst and healed, and the miles slowly fell behind them. Another Sunday arrived and they were thankful for the respite. After their chores and the religious service, people kept largely to themselves, reading their bibles and minding their own business. The euphoria that had been theirs at the beginning of the journey had worn thin and everyone was just plain tired after a hard week's drive. There was no doubt that for most, their physical health had improved immensely. With the work as demanding as it was, plus the long hours, they had shed unnecessary pounds and were more fit than they had ever been. But the other side of the coin, their psychological state, told a different story. The precept that familiarity breeds contempt sat like a vulture at the edge of the camp. People were beginning to lose their patience over petty things and easily snapped at one another. Some were particular in the way they did things while others were not; some coveted private space that others heedlessly trespassed on; some were quiet, others boisterous; and the list went on, the bottom line being that more and more often they were getting on each other's nerves.

Compounding the problem was the enormous pressure on everyone. They were, after all, in the middle of an immense wilderness, with no resources but their own should they run into any trouble. Some people handled the pressure with equanimity while others showed great strain. McMicking was certain that it was only the presence of Mrs. Schubert that kept the tempers of some of the men in check.

Catherine, meanwhile, felt stretched to the limit, with three small children to worry about in addition to her chores. Yet it was the children who helped keep her in focus, and it never ceased to amaze her how well they coped with life on the trail. They greeted each morning unburdened by the tribulations of the previous day, as if their little minds had been house-cleaned while they slept. And as long as they, in turn, were greeted by their parents, all was well in their world. Praise God if she only had half their capacity for making do. Nevertheless, she would not let the present circumstances get the best of her. She reminded herself again that she had known worse times and in that she found consolation. As she had risen above those, she would rise above these.

Sellar was feeling introspective and homesick. He'd been on the trail for two months now, yet his memory of what he had left behind was so acute that his departure sometimes seemed as if it were only yesterday. It jolted him to think of how far he'd come and exactly where he was: in a self-imposed exile somewhere on a sweeping plain, far from all the amenities of civilization, and hardest of all, far from his loved ones.

He wondered if they would even recognize him now, in his filthy pantaloons, an even filthier shirt with holes cut for ventilation, and dirty, sockless feet in tattered moccasins. Like many of the company, he'd long since given up wearing modern boots, which only hurt his feet and gave him blisters. The native footwear was far more practical and comfortable, and superior when crossing rivers and swamps. A pair would usually have to be repaired at the end of the day, and might only last for two if the terrain was rugged. But they were cheap enough and he'd bought several pairs at Fort Garry and then again at Fort Ellice.

One day Sellar and a few others shot 35 ducks, and that night for supper there was roast fowl for all who wanted it. People put their differences aside and enjoyed the feast, a welcome improvement over the steady diet of salt pork and bannock they had been subjected to for the last several days. Then the musical instruments were brought out and songs filled the evening air.

By mid-morning on June 24 the train was among the Touchwood Hills, lovely, aspen-crowned ripples in the vast carpet of the prairie, their valleys laced with small, pristine lakes. The trees were second growth, though, for it was apparent that large tracts of the forest that had once covered the hills had been lost to a devastating fire many years before. Burnt, pole-like remains of trees jutted up here and there through the rich vegetation, which also hid many more that were toppled.

Coming out of the hills, the company could see the Quill Lakes in the distance, gleaming like mercury in the heat of the day. They came to Touchwood Hills House, once an HBC trading post, but now deserted, an empty shell that was little more than a roost for cowbirds and whisky-jacks. They stopped only long enough to gorge themselves on wild strawberries and load up with firewood. By supper time, the hills were left behind as the overlanders entered a treeless plain that seemed to reach out to the very ends of the earth. It was dry and hot, and dust rose from beneath the cart wheels in billowing clouds that swirled off in the wind to dissipate in the great emptiness. An observer from afar would have seen them coming for miles. So, too, would they have been heard: the rumbling of wooden wheels over stony prairie earth, the creaking of the cart boxes, oxen bellowing, horses whinnying, human voices urging them on, sounds the land had never in its history heard in such volume. The train stretched out unbroken for more than a mile, a giant creature with a life of its own, covering the miles relatively quickly despite its size, moving inexorably closer to a place that none had ever seen and some would never see. Cariboo. It rolled off the tongue as easily as the carts rolled over the astonishingly level prairie.

For two days the landscape was as flat and hot as a stovetop. For two days the horizon was unchanging, a straight line of land and sky that looked forever unreachable. Had McMicking been asked what his definition of infinity was he would have pointed to the horizon and said, "That's it, that's as good a definition of infinity as any." In one sense he found it overwhelming, yet there was something about the limitless open space that nurtured the spirit and fed the soul, that made him feel he was in the presence of God.

They traversed a two-mile-long gravel ridge separating two large salt lakes and by Thursday, the barren plain had given way to a combination of open grasslands, brush and groves of trees. Scattered everywhere were the bones of buffalo, some bleached white by the searing sun, others brown and in varying stages of decay — gaping skulls, rib racks, large angular hip bones, all forming an enormous killing field that was beyond comprehension. How could so many animals have gathered in one spot, tens of thousands of them, and then been slaughtered? How long did it take? It was a chilling thought to McMicking, and macabre testimony to the immensity of the herds that foraged on these plains.[19]

There were sloughs in which the carts sank up to their axles, but the men were so used to them now that they plowed right through with little regard. But they still weren't used to the mosquitoes. Always troublesome, here in these wetlands the insects had become a nightmare, attacking in huge, black, nearly impenetrable swarms that filled the prairie sky and drove everyone mad. They flew into noses and ears, and God knows how many of the vile things were spat out or inadvertently swallowed. Exposed skin was covered in bites that rose in itchy red welts, often scratched so hard they bled. It was even worse for the animals, who wore the insects like a second skin, as thick as a thumb, so that one blow from a hand could kill hundreds. The men tried to help by using tree branches to fend the insects off, swishing them back and forth like cow's tails, but it was hot, hopeless work. No sooner had one cloud of mosquitoes been dispersed than another settled in its place. In camp the men built several huge smudge fires to protect the animals and themselves, and found that sleeping outside in the smoke was marginally better than being trapped inside a tent with the whining, voracious insects. Either way, sleeping was difficult so the company arose at two in the morning and moved out.

"They are as big as the hummingbirds back home, I swear," Sellar complained, "and more numerous than midges on a sand bar!"

McMicking considered Sellar's observations, if anything, to be seriously deficient.

Eventually the terrain grew gravelly and hilly and the mosquitoes lessened to a tolerable level.

McMicking was pleased with the way things were going. Despite the interpersonal problems, discipline and order in the company were tremendously improved and it now operated with the precision of a drill team. When the cry "Every man to his ox!" was heard in the morning, the animals were harnessed, everything was loaded, and the entire train was under way in 15 minutes. The Huntingdon men had to be thanked for that. Though their ambition had caused friction within the company, it was the catalyst that got everyone working together. Now routine had turned into rhythm and the days played out like a symphony.

The early hours were the best time to travel. The air was relatively cool and refreshing and the insects were less menacing, sometimes non-existent. It was the time that McMicking enjoyed most, when he was filled with energy and ready to accept the challenges of the coming day. And there always seemed to be something. If it wasn't insects, rain or mud, it was the sun.

One morning it boasted of its intensity as soon as it appeared above the horizon. As it climbed toward noon, first orange, then white hot, it saturated the earth with its heat, and when the earth could hold no more it sent the heat back. Shimmering waves rose from the ground to form a torrid sea that soaked in sweat all those who waded through it, sucking strength from limbs, so that every movement required monumental effort. It was all a man could do to haul out his neckerchief and wipe his brow so that his eyes would cease stinging from the salt water streaming into them. Clothes rubbed against skin like wood rasps. Feet in leather boots might just as well have been encased in hot coals. And then it got hotter. By the time the sun was past its zenith, descriptions such as furnace, cauldron or forge would not have been regarded as hyperbole. Even the wind that inevitably rose in the afternoon did nothing to ease the misery. The heat became more than something to be tolerated. It had to be survived.

As the cart train passed along a wide valley beside the Minichinas Hills, Catherine, astride her buckskin mare, felt a headache gathering behind her eyes. It was from the heat, and the wicked dust that blocked her sinuses so badly that she could only breathe through her mouth. She sought relief by drifting back to some of the happier moments of her early childhood among the cool mountains of Mourne. Praise God if the mountains of British Columbia are half as inviting! Even the hand-woven straw hat she'd bought in Fort Garry seemed glued to her head. She would rip it off if she didn't think that her brains would boil. She shifted in the saddle to ease the heat and the stickiness and numbness of her buttocks. Her lips were badly chapped, and she needed to make a balm for them at the first opportunity. There was movement inside her more and more often now, and she was beginning to have doubts that they would reach Cariboo before the baby put in an appearance. They'd been on the trail a month and had covered only a third of the distance. And from what she'd been led to understand, this was the easy part of the trail. Beyond Fort Edmonton it was, apparently, a different kettle of fish.

At each day's end the company registered the miles covered. Slow progress meant about 20 miles, good progress about 30. Complaints arose one night in camp that the miles being logged were inaccurate. James Wattie, who had taken on the responsibility for the task, was unfazed by the assertions. "I know when I've walked a mile," he said, "and I'll prove it." The next day a surveyor's chain, 66 feet in length, was used to measure accurately the distance that Wattie paced off. The train started off with Wattie walking in the lead. In a while he called out "Mile one!" He was eight feet short. Later, "Mile two!" Forty-two feet long. Then, "Mile three!" Twelve feet short. He was checked against the chain for 14 miles and was so close the figures weren't worth disputing. The chain was put away.

They camped beside another alkaline lake because it was the only thing wet that the land had to offer. The animals were looking worn, and McMicking wondered how they kept going day after day as they did, pulling such heavy loads. Thank goodness there was usually plenty of grass for them to feed on. The energy of the company was all but sapped. A lot of miles had been covered, some requiring back-breaking work, all demanding a degree of discipline and focus that most of the men had never had to call upon in their entire lives. Tempers were short, exacerbated by the heat, and the evenings were sometimes filled with petty quarrels and bickering. Beyond Catherine's hearing, there was a good deal of cursing as men changed work partners because they couldn't get along or lost faith in one another. Fatigue, though, would usually intervene and most were wearily wrapping themselves in blankets inside tents and beneath tarpaulins sloping down from carts before daylight gave way to darkness.

Fortunately, there were Sundays to ease the tension, when the burden of the trail was cast off and the strain to move forward was temporarily put aside. It was a day that underlined the laws of moral obligation and reminded men of the need to be good to one another. More than a day of rest, Sunday was a cementer of relationships, a soother of the mind, a comfort to the body and an elixir for the soul. Sunday was the linchpin that held the company together.

And that was why, on Sunday, June 29, when it was suggested that they move on to the South Saskatchewan River because it couldn't be more than a few miles away, and it would be good to be there at first light, ready to cross, a majority of the company voted it down.

Instead, they were up by a quarter past one in the morning, invigorated by the obstacle that awaited them and the break in the routine of plodding forward. Some swore they could smell the river, even above the animals and themselves. The company was moving within ten minutes of the call to oxen, and by 3:30 the first carts had reached the tree- and grass-covered bluffs above the South Saskatchewan. One by one the others arrived until they were all gathered like an army awaiting daybreak and the signal to attack.

At the first hint of dawn McMicking walked down a long coulee to the river bank. Before him, in varying shades of grey and black, was the south branch of the great river that he'd heard and read so much about. It held almost mythological proportions in his mind, and made him think of men like La Vérendrye, who discovered it, and David Thompson, who explored it. Especially Thompson, who had died in Montreal just five years ago. He also thought about drowning. The dream had returned again last night, brought on, he supposed, by his apprehension of crossing the river. Once more he had awakened gasping for air. He didn't understand the dreams, which drew him deep within himself and made him worry more than was reasonable. He saw them as a major flaw in his character. He let go a sigh and tried to relax. The mind was its own place, and could make a heaven of Hell and a hell of Heaven. Milton had said that, and he was right.

For a change, the grade to the river was gentle. The trail ran straight as a city street across a grassy field, among poplar groves, then down through a broad coulee into a thick tangle of trees lining the muddy, swirling river.[20] It was 300 yards to the far shore and, as luck would have it, that's where the ferry was tied up. Alexander Robertson and another man stripped and swam the river to retrieve it.

While some of the company breakfasted, others prepared for the crossing. Six carts at a time were taken down to the water's edge. There, the oxen were unharnessed, the goods unloaded, and the wheels removed. The ferry was a *bateau*, otherwise known as a York boat, a flat-bottomed vessel with a steeply pitched bow and stern that the HBC used to transport furs and general goods along the river. It was large enough to accommodate everything except the animals, which had to be swum across. While the vessel was being rowed over, six more carts were made ready.

Many of the animals found the river intimidating, and obstinately refused to enter. They had to be forced in, a task made easier by the fact that there was no place, beyond the trail, to which they could escape. Once in the water, most of them simply milled around until someone jumped in to keep them moving in the right direction.

James Kelso, astride his horse and working a span of oxen into the river, felt uneasy. He was a 28-year-old from Acton, a farming community northwest of Toronto, and this was not a role in which he had ever imagined himself. Born in Scotland, he had emigrated to New York where he worked as a bookkeeper, but when he fell ill, a doctor told him that the woods of Canada were a much healthier place in which to live. On the strength of that advice he went north and ended up in Acton. When news of the gold strikes in Cariboo arrived, and an overland party was formed, he joined without hesitation. The possibilities of untold wealth and adventure were irresistible, but so far there had been more hard work than adventure. Now he had to herd these animals across the fabled South Saskatchewan River, and he wasn't sure of himself. The oxen had gone out several yards, but the deepening water and the pull of the current frightened them, and they began to turn back. Kelso spurred his horse into the river to redirect them.

In a trice he was in deep water and the horse was no longer supporting him. Foolishly, he let go of the reins. He had dressed warmly for the cool morning and his layered clothing absorbed the cold water like a sponge, growing so leaden that swimming was impossible. He tried to roll over on his back, but the weight of his clothes pulled him under. Fighting to keep his head above water, he cried for help, choking and flailing arms that even in his panicked state felt as heavy as anvils. He thought that he heard men on the shore shouting, but wasn't sure, his mind was so jumbled. Then someone was swimming toward him but he couldn't hold on. The river filled his ears, his mouth and his nose, and he didn't care any more. Blackness wrapped him in a cold shroud.

The men he'd heard on the shore were non-swimmers, and all they could do was add to the drowning man's cries for help. They sounded an alarm so loud it could be heard back on the bluff where others of the company were awaiting their turn. Three men — George Reid, William Strachan and William Phillips — raced to the river. Reid, the stronger of the three, quickly stripped down and plunged in, swimming as fast as his arms and thrashing feet would propel him. Just as he neared Kelso, the young Scot disappeared, going under for the last time. Reid dove beneath the surface, unable to see a thing, but by a stroke of good luck bumped into him. With a strength he didn't realize he possessed, he grabbed the drowning man by the neck of his coat and brought him to the surface. Then he towed him toward shore, sucking in air that never seemed quite enough, until Strachan and Phillips could help drag him the rest of the way.

Kelso was unconscious, and looked as if the last breath had gone from him. Strachan squeezed gouts of water out of his lungs until it was replaced by air, and colour returned to his face. When Kelso opened his eyes and saw his rescuers above him and the trees and sky behind, he wondered, in his confusion, why Heaven was so similar to the earthly plane. Then it dawned on him that he'd been brought back from the brink of death.

Once the crisis was past, the business of getting the cart train across the river continued throughout the long day. Like an assembly line, the carts and oxen came down the hill in sixes on one side, crossed the river, then went up the hill in sixes on the other. By five o'clock, the last boatload had crossed and all the animals had been taken over.

The Schuberts and their democrat wagon were among the last to cross. For Catherine, her main task had been keeping the children entertained throughout the day while they awaited their turn. It was the first time Gus Jr. had been on a boat and to his six-year-old eyes the river seemed as wide as forever. During the crossing he asked his mother, "Is this the ocean, Ma?"

"It only seems that way," Catherine answered, "but it's just a river, and thanks be to God that it is, for the ocean is no place for a vessel the likes of this."

Sellar and the Huntingdon men, who had crossed the river before noon, continued on to Fort Carlton, some 20 miles farther, while McMicking, who oversaw the entire operation, and those who had crossed in the afternoon, corralled the animals a mile down the trail from the river and set up camp. His feelings were mixed. On the one hand he was elated that another barrier on the trail, the biggest one so far, had been crossed. On the other, he was anxious over almost losing a man in the process. That it could just as easily have been he himself was disconcerting in the extreme. So was the fact that the north branch of this magnificent river was only 20 miles away, and it too would have to be crossed.

By eleven o'clock on Tuesday morning, July 1, the tail end of the company had descended the poplar bluff overlooking Fort Carlton, a small rectangle of timber uprights with corner bastions and several small buildings inside them. It was a lovely spot, on the east bank of the North Saskatchewan River, with about 50 acres of the surrounding area cultivated. Inside the stockade, the uneven ground, churned up during the last heavy rain, had dried as hard as stone. There appeared to be more dogs around than humans, more Métis, half-breeds, and Indians than whites, and more dog feces than all of those put together.

McMicking, after consulting with the HBC factor, was relieved to learn that the trail to Fort Pitt, another 150 miles to the northwest, was well marked. They paid the man 12½¢ per cart for the use of the *bateaux* on both rivers, bought some fresh buffalo meat that had just arrived at the fort that morning, then headed down to the river for their second major crossing in two days.

The north branch of the Saskatchewan was a little broader than its southern counterpart, but nowhere near as deep. Sandbars poked up here and there along its visible length and this lifted McMicking's spirit. He ran the same routine they had used on the south branch, and by nightfall they were all safely across, except for three oxen which were swept away downstream and never recovered.

Sellar and his group were waiting at the campsite, having crossed the river just as McMicking and the others were arriving at the fort. He and his companions had spent their idle time writing letters to loved ones, which someone took back to Fort Carlton to mail.

During the afternoon, huge, anvil-topped clouds had built up on the horizon, and by late evening the wind moaned under the great burden of a storm. The fiery bursts that were once harmless in the distance were now overhead. Thunder crashed and lightning flashed almost simultaneously as the wind roared through, its ferocity driving the overlanders outside to hang on to their tents for fear of losing them. Hail pelted them like someone hurling handfuls of pebbles. Others, afraid to be exposed in such a storm, were hiding beneath the carts, wondering if they all might be blown away. Some were prone on the sopping ground to make themselves less of a target for the lightning, but a few saw it as a game played by the gods, and peals of childlike laughter were heard between the thunderclaps and above the bellowing of the oxen from the corral. By the time the storm was spent enough to reset the tents for sleeping, it was almost time to get up.

As a result, they got away late the next morning, under a clearing sky but with the wind still gusting strongly. For the time being the squabbles had ceased and there was much good feeling among the company. Four major obstacles had been met and conquered. They were a well-honed unit and everyone, including Catherine, was stronger, tougher, trimmer and more resilient than ever before. And now they knew, with a confidence that had taken some time to build, that they were capable of meeting whatever hardships the trail ahead had to offer. They had not come here to be defeated, and they would not be.

The North Saskatchewan River now flowed out of the southwest while the cart train headed northwest. They would meet up again in about 125 miles. As the river disappeared from view, the character of the countryside underwent a striking change. There were more hills now, more trees, and the soil was sandy and loose. A strong wind persisted from the north; it picked up the loose soil, scoured everyone with stinging clouds of dust, and obscured the hills. Their mouths were dry, their tongues coated, and when they drank from their canteens, they spat the gritty water out rather than swallow it. The cart wheels sank in the sand as if it were mud and added considerable strain to the oxen's workload. They forded a small river three feet deep, with a muddy bottom, and camped for the night after making 28 hard-fought miles.

The next day conditions deteriorated further. Not only was the ground still rough, but it was cut through with steep gullies and ropes were required to let the carts down one side and pull them up the other. The stoicism with which the company handled these obstacles was rewarded, for after this their lot improved markedly. The land was now veined with clear, swift-flowing creeks of cool, sweet water that seemed like small miracles compared to the brackish lake and slough water they had been forced to drink on the flatlands east of the South Saskatchewan. The air was cooler too, and that was a welcome relief. Through the Thickwood Hills, the weather remained favourable, with only infrequent rain showers, and they stopped one night in an enormous field of wild strawberries. Every available container was filled to the brim, and that evening, after supper, the cows were milked and everyone dined like royalty on strawberries and fresh cream.

That same evening Eustache Pattison and Bill Irwin of the Huntingdon party rode out about ten miles from camp looking for bear, but found none. On their way back, Pattison dismounted to shoot a crow, and his horse wandered off. Irwin tried to catch it, but maddeningly, the animal trotted off every time it was approached. Since it appeared to be going in the general direction of camp the two men decided that Irwin would follow along to make sure it got there, while Pattison started walking. They both reasoned that camp couldn't be too far away.

Watching his friend disappear over a low rise caused Pattison's stomach to turn. The utter silence and solitude were almost terrifying. He struck out, over the same rise, then another and another, but camp was obviously much farther away than he supposed. He began to wonder if he was walking in the right direction. If not, he was probably at least headed in the general direction of the cart trail, and when he crossed it, he should be able to find camp from there. But sundown approached and he had seen no recognizable landmarks. Now he worried that he might miss the trail completely in the dark. He stopped and, gathering up some dried buffalo dung, lit a fire. He'd stay put for the night. The notion occurred to him that if he wasn't lost then this was as close as he ever wanted to come to it. And if he was, and couldn't find his way back to the others, it would be hard to imagine a more lonely place in which to die. He shouted "Hello!" just in case there was help nearby, and was startled when someone fired a revolver in response. He shouted several times more, and soon two riders appeared over a rise. In ten minutes he was back in the safety of the camp. No one had doubted that he would find his way back, but they had become concerned as night fell. A larger party had already volunteered to search for him at first light.

Leaving the hills the next day the company realized it was being followed. Not by Indians, but by packs of timber wolves. With the buffalo gone south for the season there were no herds for the wolves to prey on, so they followed the overlanders, watching every move, looking for any signs of weakness that would provide an opening for an attack. Catherine kept a closer watch on the children, especially little Gus, who was allowed to wander through the camp after supper. At night the wolves set up a chorus of howls that continued till the early hours when the company arose. Many found it nerve-wracking at first, but like everything else, they eventually got used to it.

They moved on, through a slough that reached the top of the cart boxes, soaking everything and spoiling some of the supplies. Catherine was so badly chilled she donned as much clothing as she could in a vain effort to get warm. She had only just dried out when she was soaked again crossing another river. It wasn't a big one, but there was no timber around to build a bridge, so the cart wheels had to be removed and the boxes floated across. Beyond the river the trail improved greatly, passing through a fine, rolling country punctuated with stands of poplar. When there wasn't any water to cross, the travelling was easy. They arrived at Jackfish Lake in time to spend the Sabbath on its shore. Its beauty reminded them of Shoal Lake, and the abundance of fish brought a timely, albeit temporary, break in a steady diet of pemmican and salt pork.

With the Sabbath well-kept, the company was refreshed and energetic. It was a hospitable country they were now passing through, with so few challenges that the daily routine became tedious. One afternoon, in lunch camp, Sellar proposed a cart race. The idea excited several of the men, who leapt to their feet demanding to be entrants. Some even offered bets. Soon, more than two dozen carts formed up along a line, and McMicking fired a rifle shot to begin the race. Despite the wide expanse of the prairie, the carts crowded each other and some became so entangled they ground to a halt. Others upset from their excessive speed over the uneven terrain, and their loads were scattered helter-skelter. There was no clear winner, but it was such good fun that when Fort Pitt was predicted to be only 25 miles away, they raced the entire distance to it. Sellar and the Huntingdon men beat their closest rival by one hour, and the slowest of the company by a full day. Few had expected any other outcome.

The fort, a low palisade enclosing a half-dozen buildings, sat on a bench 20 feet above the North Saskatchewan River, with a hill sloping upward behind it. The only signs of cultivation were a field of wheat on one side, and one of potatoes on the other. Nevertheless, to the overlanders it was another island of civilization in an otherwise empty prairie sea.

Everyone took advantage of the break to make general repairs to the carts, bake bread and write letters home. McMicking traded one of his oxen for a horse, and a cart for some butter and fresh buffalo meat. Another man traded his dog and a silver watch for a horse, a good dog being highly valued here. Alexander Fortune accepted an invitation to dine at the home of a Highland Scot, an old family friend. Later, when McMicking asked what he'd had for dinner, Fortune said, "Buffalo meat stewed, buffalo meat boiled, and buffalo steak; and to drink we had Saskatchewan River water with sediment flowing through it!"

The fort's factor had a warning for the overlanders. "This is the end of the good trail from the east," he said. "Most of the travelling between here and Fort Edmonton is by *bateau*, rather than overland, so there's not much of a trail to follow on either side of the river. If you are determined to carry on regardless, then I strongly suggest you hire a guide. There's a good man here at the fort that I would highly recommend. His name is Michel Callihoo."

McMicking called a general meeting to discuss, among other things, procuring a guide. There were concerns that the area between Forts Pitt and Edmonton was rife with Indian wars. A few days earlier Indians had captured some white men, and though the captives weren't killed, they did lose their clothes, and were sent back to the fort naked. The discussion of this incident was followed by some new rules.

1st, that all guns be cleaned and kept in first order and ready for action at short notice.

2nd, that Captain McMicking should be colonel of the expedition.

3rd, that Alexander Robertson be made captain.

4th, that the company should be divided into four companies for travelling convenience.

5th, that the whole company should travel in close order, to prevent the Indians from attacking the centre of the train and dividing it.

6th, that the service of a guide be procured to guide [them] to Edmonton.[21]

Afterwards, McMicking, Robertson and a few others met with Callihoo to feel him out. He was an Iroquois Indian, but had been in the west since he was a youngster, working for the fur traders as a hunter and trapper. The men listened as he recommended the southern trail — that is, what there was of a trail — over the northern one. "Not because it's easier," he said, "but because it's shorter. Other than distance there is not much to choose between them. If you're concerned about problems with Indians, you needn't worry. The Blackfeet have gone south, on the trail of the buffalo, and any stray bands that might be left would think twice before attacking a caravan as large and fully armed as yours."

Callihoo was well spoken and quietly confident; nevertheless, the overlanders were faced with a tough decision. Having been burned badly once they were feeling somewhat mistrustful, because if this guide's information was incorrect and he deserted them out where the trail was mostly indiscernible, they could be in serious trouble. They dismissed Callihoo for a moment to confer with each other.

"What say you, Tom?" Robertson asked.

"It's difficult not to think of Racette in these circumstances," McMicking replied, "but we shouldn't allow our experience with him to colour our impressions of Callihoo. He seems competent enough, and I can't see that we have any reasonable alternative. If we go guideless and the trail is faint, what happens if the weather turns sour? We might be doomed. If we wait for another guide to come along — and that might be days or weeks — how will we know if we can trust him? Besides, we can't wait that long. I say we take our chances with Callihoo."

Everyone agreed. Calling Callihoo back, McMicking related the problems they had had with Racette, the lack of communication in particular. He stressed the importance of maintaining close contact with him, as colonel, and no one else. "It is a great responsibility that we ask of you. If you have any doubts that you might not be able to fulfill it, then speak now. Otherwise, it is our expectation that you will see this company through to Fort Edmonton, and that you will not desert simply because it becomes convenient for you to do so."

The guide held out his hand to McMicking. "I am Callihoo," he said, "not Racette."

Taking the southern route meant crossing the North Saskatchewan again, but the company had river crossing down pat and accomplished the task in short order and without difficulty. Once they were all on the south shore, camp was made for the night. McMicking was too apprehensive to find sleep right away. He worried about the decision to hire Callihoo, whether it was the right one, and whether he, Robertson and the others had simply signed an open death warrant. He especially worried about Catherine Schubert and the children. He had never met a more admirable woman, but the trail to Fort Edmonton, though only 150 miles, crossed a land that was little travelled and potentially hostile. And no one, not even the guide, could predict what it might hold in store for them.

The first two days passed pleasantly enough, although it seemed as if they could have crossed the country stepping on buffalo dung, without ever touching the ground. Of the beasts themselves there was nary a sign. Callihoo said they had migrated to the flatlands farther south and would not return to this area and the shelter of the hills and trees until the onset of winter. A couple of antelope were encountered, though, and several of the company gave chase just for the fun of it. The animals, however, were much too alert and fast to be caught. A large wolf, one of several that had been following the train to scavenge on the garbage left behind, ventured too close to the camp and was shot. Then on Friday afternoon the sky, which had been darkening all day, let loose a torrent of rain. It poured through the night and all day Saturday. On Sunday it was still pouring. Some tarps were rigged up for the religious service, but everyone was so wet it hardly mattered. By Monday the rain still hadn't let up and most of the company wanted to stay put. There was a meeting about this but McMicking and Callihoo vetoed the idea. If they were ever going to make Fort Edmonton, they would have to ignore the weather and push on regardless. But even as they spoke, the interminable rain was beginning to create other problems.

They reached the Vermilion River and crossed it easily enough by making rafts from two cart wheels tied together and lined underneath with tents and rubber blankets. Then they strung a line across the river and pulled the rafts, loaded with supplies, back and forth along it. That done, they floated the carts over and swam the animals across. But beyond the Vermilion, many of the small streams that were also tributaries of the North Saskatchewan were flooding so badly they could no longer be forded. The men hacked down trees when they were available and built crude bridges — eight in four days, one nearly a hundred feet long. Near one overflowing creek, as luck would have it, there wasn't a tree in sight. The wheels from some of the lead carts were removed and the boxes sunk in the creek, enough to form a makeshift roadbed, and the rest of the train crossed over.

Like a biblical flood the water spread out before them as they traversed 10 to 12 sloughs a day. One was a mile wide and two feet deep, with another foot of mud beneath the water. The only thing that kept the company from sinking out of sight was the long buffalo grass growing in the slough.

And so it went. Day after day they plodded on, up and down hills, through mudholes, across creeks and sloughs, wading in water up to their knees, up to their waists, up to their chins, or sometimes just plain swimming. Rain poured from hat brims like small rivers. Many got tired of their heavy, water-soaked clothes and stripped down to their underwear, even though the water was bitterly cold. Everyone's feet were raw from being wet for so long. And though the rain would temporarily let up now and then, any notion that this might be a land route had been cynically set aside. It was more like a vast inland sea, and *bateaux* might have been a more efficient mode of transportation. During one lunch stop there wasn't a dry stick to be seen anywhere so one of the men cut up his storage box for firewood.

Catherine found it impossible to keep the children dry and worried that they would catch their death of colds. With their supplies dwindling, Augustus was able to clear a small space in the back of the democrat for Gus Jr. and Mary Jane, beneath the tarp. It was a jolting ride but at least they were dry. James was too tiny to withstand the wagon's erratic movement and was kept in his basket. Catherine covered him as best she could but as she grumbled to Augustus later, "If there's a hole for water to seep into, it'll soon be after finding it."

The campgrounds at night, despite being on higher ground, were always soaked and spongy, and offered no real chance to dry out. At one camp, some feared that the water would rise overnight so they took the precaution of removing the sideboards that extended the height of the carts, and using them as platforms on which to make their beds. Sellar and his tent-mates went even further and built a platform of brush two feet high, put their boards on top of that, then fit the floorless tent over the structure. Headroom inside the tent was reduced substantially but there was still enough space to maneuver. They then placed their rubber blankets, buffalo robes and wool blankets on top of the platform, to make a dry, comfortable bed. Meanwhile, the Schuberts erected a shelter on the back of the wagon and made themselves as comfortable as they could on top of their supplies. That evening the rain began at nine and sheeted down like a waterfall all night. Come morning, everything was afloat except Sellar, his mates and the Schuberts, who had all slept dry. Nevertheless, almost everything they and the company owned was wet and mildewed.

Everyone was soaked clear to the bone, saturated, and in such a state of exhaustion that they would not have argued if someone said the world had always been like this. So consumed were they by their present state of affairs they found it impossible to recall, even momentarily, those dry, hot days west of the Touchwood Hills, when the prairie seemed limitless and it was sweat that rolled down their faces, not rainwater. Now the horizon was hidden by precipitation and low angry clouds that reduced the world to almost claustrophobic proportions. They encountered fog, too, and Callihoo became slightly confused about where they were. Some of the more philosophical among the company muttered that bad things couldn't exist forever, anymore than a man could. Still, it rained on 11 consecutive days, and their progress had slowed to a crawl. Some days they were lucky to make 20 miles. Concerned for the company's morale, McMicking insisted that whenever possible, musical instruments be brought out and played. Although he hadn't much of a voice, he led everyone in song. "Fill the night with music," he quoted to them, "and the cares that infest the day shall fold their tents like the Arabs, and as silently steal away."[22]

These evenings were a light in the gloom for some, but had just the opposite effect on others and made them homesick. In their dreams the glitter of gold had been replaced by the faces of wives and children, all the loved ones left behind in a far-off place called "home," the existence of which had become a matter of faith.

The company was waiting out the rain one afternoon when someone spotted a dozen or more human figures just below the crest of a rise. A general alarm spread through the camp. It had to be a band of Blackfeet and, for all they knew, the vanguard of hundreds more to follow. A small panic gripped the men as they scrambled for their weapons and prepared them for firing. Callihoo mounted and rode out to assess the situation. He had not gone far before he turned back, a smile on his face. The band of Indians was nothing more than a few stunted trees swaying in the wind. The good news loosened the tension, but the incident served as a reminder that weapons should be kept oiled and handy at all times.

McMicking was pleased with the decision to hire Callihoo, and knew that the rest of the company was too. The guide had proven himself a dozen times since Fort Pitt, especially in this inclement weather when the rain and flooding had obliterated whatever trail might have existed in the first place. The man's sense of direction was uncanny, even through the fog. He got turned around once but who wouldn't have? For certain, the company would have been hopelessly lost without him. This latest incident was just another example of his worth. Had those bushes turned out to be Blackfeet, Callihoo spoke their language, and in all probability would have gained the cart train safe passage.

Later that day they passed through a meadow containing several hundred tethering posts and the remains of a dead horse, not yet picked clean by carrion eaters. "It's a battlefield," said Callihoo, "and fairly recent. Blackfeet and Cree."

Sellar remarked that if the company had not been held up by the rain, and had passed this way earlier, there might have been an occasion to practise the art of war. It was a thought that both frightened and excited him, and seemed somehow to be a reasonable alternative to the drudgery of life on the trail.

McMicking did not like the feeling that Sellar's words stirred within him, but said only, "War is not an art, Jim. It's an illness in the hearts of men, savage and civilized alike."

On Sunday, July 20, the overlanders were forced to do the one thing they hoped they would never have to do — travel on their day of rest. However, it looked as if the rain was going to flood them out of their campsite and it might be best to move to higher ground. There were few complaints, but en route, another bridge needed to be built. A group led by Alexander Fortune protested.

"It's enough that we've violated our Sabbath rules by travelling. We should not add insult to injury by working. Surely the task can wait till tomorrow!"

"Tomorrow might be too late," said McMicking. "If we don't cross now, it could be days before we're able to. That would not only be foolish, but it could prove dangerous as well. We all know that we haven't made as much progress as we expected and food supplies are running low. What we decide here may very well determine whether we make it to Fort Edmonton or not."

Fortune was adamant. "We will trust the God of the Sabbath, who also rules the floods!"

It bothered McMicking to have to argue with this pious man; indeed the very idea of breaking the Sabbath pained him. But these were unusual circumstances that called for unusual measures. "I'm sure the good Lord would not see us starve to death for the want of building a small bridge."

Sellar nodded. Though a long-time acquaintance of Fortune's —
both were Huntingdon men — and opposed to Sunday travel himself,
his practical side won out. "Let's build the bridge now, Alex," he said,
"and then give over to God whatever remains of the day."

Fortune and his followers refused to be part of the impiety.
They would go no farther on this day, and they watched as the
rest of the company went to work building the bridge. Once it
was finished and the crossing commenced, a few of the men who
had backed Fortune had a change of heart and crossed over
themselves, fearing that the bridge might wash out overnight.
The Schuberts crossed as well, the safety of the children foremost
in their minds. Not Fortune, though. He stayed put, and called
those who deserted him the worst thing he could think of:
"Sabbath breakers!"

That night Sellar and another man were out for a walk when
they came to a knoll rising about 150 feet above the surrounding
terrain. Hoping they might catch a glimpse of the fort, they
climbed to the top. Edmonton was nowhere to be seen.
Nevertheless, the view was almost as rewarding. Despite the
lowering, sombre sky, they could see for miles in all directions,
and about four or five miles to the north, twisting into the distance
like a beige snake, was the North Saskatchewan River, seen for
the first time since they had left Fort Pitt. The sight heartened
them, for it meant they were nearing their goal. And stretching
down the slope before them were broad meadows of wild
raspberries, some as big as plums. The two men stuffed themselves
and filled their hats, then headed back to camp to share their
exciting discoveries with the others.

It scarcely rained during the night, and the bridge was still
standing in the morning. Fortune had been right. They could

have given the entire Sabbath over to God and waited till Monday to build the bridge. He and the others broke camp and self-righteously crossed over.

Sellar watched from the far side and seethed. Words welled up inside him, but they found no voice. Sure, Fortune could call him a Sabbath breaker, but what was Fortune? He was a thief who stole the labour of others, plain and simple, and that was even worse. The knowledge of that helped ease Sellar's own feelings of guilt and gave him some satisfaction.

"Mr. Fortune's not a practical man," Catherine told Augustus as they loaded up the democrat, "but he's lucky, I'll give you that." Her husband was in ill-humour and only grunted. A toothache had been building in his right upper jaw all morning and he was more concerned about it than that damned fool Fortune. He asked Catherine to dig out the oil of cloves from their medicine kit.

The company crossed more creeks during the next day, and the rain came intermittently. Visibility was poor. At six in the evening, they were brought to halt by a ravine that cut across their path, 200 feet deep, with a creek surging along its bottom. The east side was steep and tree-lined, the west bank more gently sloped and open. The men cut a trail down through the trees and used what they had fallen to build a bridge. Then they began the onerous task of lowering the carts into the ravine by ropes. Luckily, the oxen were able to get enough of a purchase on the far side to pull the carts up themselves.

McMicking was deeply satisfied with the way the men set to the task and especially the way they helped each other. The seeds of co-operation that had been planted at the meeting back near the Qu'Appelle were bearing good fruit, despite the small irritations that occurred from time to time. He saw it as his responsibility to ensure that this spirit was maintained through to the end of the journey.

Had she been asked, Catherine Schubert would have freely admitted to being the chief beneficiary of this co-operative spirit. She never had to worry about getting the children safely over the rivers and sloughs, and deep ravines like this one. Peter Marlowe, a Huntingdon man with one of the strongest horses, was particularly helpful in this regard. In every instance he volunteered his services without being asked. In camp, when circumstances permitted, he loved to look after the children, and other men, probably missing children at home, would often help entertain them. Tom Murphy, from Queenston, was a master storyteller, and mesmerized Gus Jr. and Mary Jane with tales of pirates and derring-do. It warmed Catherine's heart to be among so many good men. She could not imagine what the journey would have been like if she and her family had tried it on their own. They might not have made it this far.

The company set up camp on the far side of the ravine, exhausted from the long day's toil. McMicking was worried. Where was Fort Edmonton, anyway? Even Callihoo was beginning to wonder if they might have passed it in the foul weather. What if each step they were taking was actually leading them farther and farther from their goal? It was too dispiriting for further contemplation, considering that every one of those steps demanded such tremendous effort.

Sellar, indefatigable and active, was not about to sit around and fret, and after supper he rode out to scout the trail ahead. There were still too many idlers in the company as far as he was concerned. Perhaps not as many as before, but enough that it still bothered him. He would have demanded more from them had it been within his power to do so. He moved off, giving his horse its head through the trees, splashed across a small creek, and a few moments later went up over a small rise that ended in a bluff. At first, he could not believe his eyes. There before him was the North Saskatchewan, and a hundred feet above it, on the far side, Fort Edmonton. He drank in the sight, let it fill his senses to overflowing, as if to verify that it wasn't a mirage, then whipped his horse around and raced back to camp, clods of mud flying up in every direction. Reining up he shouted, "Fort Edmonton! The fort is just ahead!"

The company, abuzz with excitement, quickly broke camp, pulling their tents down and throwing them, along with other supplies, in jumbled heaps into the carts. Everything was so wet no one bothered to douse fires. They moved out in record time, and followed Sellar's lead to the bluff above the river. It was less than a quarter of a mile.

They had done it! They were bedraggled and hurting, rubbed raw, soaked and spent, but they'd done it! They had reached the first goal they'd set for themselves in Fort Garry, 900 miles behind them, and now stood on the very threshold of Eldorado. As weary as they were, their exhilaration was palpable. There was handshaking and backslapping all around, and all the petty grievances were vanquished by the euphoria of the moment. They gave thanks, not only to Providence for making this possible, but also to Michel Callihoo to whom a part of the victory must surely belong. Only God knew where they would be on this day without him.

At dawn, the Union Jack was raised over the fort and a cannon fired to salute the arrival of the overlanders. In response, the company raised the English standard that they had brought with them from the east, and fired a 21-gun salute. But they would not see the inside of the fort on this day, nor on the next.

Such was the extent of the flooding in the area that all the HBC boats had been washed 15 miles down river, and the company had to wait two days before enough were retrieved to ferry everyone across. Yet most didn't mind the wait. Neither the rain nor the temporary obstacle in their path could dampen their enthusiasm. The mere sight of the sprawling structure sustained them.[23] And when at last they had attained the far shore and were making their way up the long slope to the stockade gate, they walked with their shoulders erect and their heads up, with a pride befitting their awesome passage.

The Road to Tête Jaune Cache

Does the road wind uphill all the way?
Yes, to the very end.
Will the day's journey take the whole long day?
From morn to night, my friend.

Christina Rossetti, "Uphill"

Fort Edmonton to Tête Jaune Cache
July 26 — August 31, 1862

Fort Edmonton, though built of wood, was on a par with Fort Garry as far as size and importance were concerned, and was the hub of these far western plains. In addition to its role in the fur trade and as a provisions depot for travellers, it was where most of the boats plying the river had been built, and it boasted of one feature that Fort Garry could not: the "Big House," otherwise known as "Rowand's Folly." It stood three storeys high, measured 30 feet wide by 80 feet long, and was chock-a-block with small-paned windows. Porches trimmed both the front and rear. Inside, in addition to Rowand's living quarters, were a gentlemen's mess and the only ballroom in the Northwest.

Later that evening McMicking, dry at last, sat in the gentlemen's mess with George Brazeau, temporary master of the fort, while William Christie was away, and over some of the HBC's finest brandy, listened eagerly to the story of the house's builder.

"John Rowand," Brazeau said, "was the Chief Factor here from 1823 to 1854, and the Company has not seen the likes of him since. He was a huge man in both size and personality. The fort was suffering financially when he arrived but he soon had it showing a profit again. One of the first things he did was impress the Indians with the Company's importance by building the Big House. They had never seen a building so large, and they'd never seen glass before. He'd had it imported in molasses barrels to prevent breakage and the Indians were completely enthralled by it.

"As a young man he was stationed at Fort des Prairies and one day, when he was out riding alone, the horse threw him. He broke his leg and couldn't move. Luckily, a young country-born woman had seen him go off and was concerned when his horse returned riderless. The animal led her to Rowand and she managed to get him back to the fort where she cared for him until he was fully recovered. Her name was Louise, and he married her a short time later."

Brazeau sipped some brandy, then continued. "They both loved parties and held many here in the Big House. They also shared a

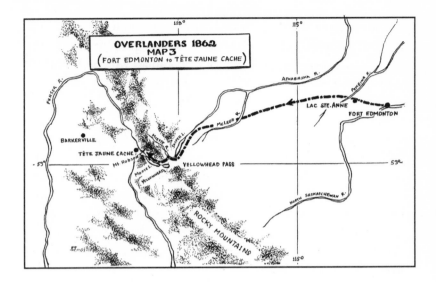

love of food and, like Rowand, Louise weighed well over 300 pounds. Their daughter Margaret was even heavier, and when the three of them were on the same floor it creaked and groaned in protest. The servants below were afraid that the family would crash through!

"He was not a man to tolerate idlers. Apparently, he would tell his servants, whenever they complained of being ill, that if they weren't dead within three days then there probably wasn't much wrong with them in the first place.

"In 1854, Rowand was on his way down the North Saskatchewan on furlough when he stopped in at Fort Pitt. The first thing he saw was two Métis having a fight, which was something else he wouldn't tolerate, so he rushed in to break them up. I guess the excitement was too much for him because he dropped dead from a heart attack.

"He was buried at Fort Pitt but he'd requested in his will that his final resting-place be Montreal, where he grew up. So a year later they dug up his body and had an Indian woman boil the rotting flesh from his bones. Her reward for putting up with the stink was that she got to keep the fat. I understand she made soap from it."

McMicking grimaced and Brazeau, obviously enjoying the effect, went on. "Anyway, the bones were put inside a partly full rum keg to preserve them and an order was issued to take the keg to Fort Garry, and then on to Montreal. But a storm blew up on Lake Winnipeg and the container ended up in the water. By a stroke of blind luck it was found, but was taken to York Factory instead of Fort Garry. As you probably know, York Factory is on Hudson Bay and the best way to get from there to Montreal is by way of England, so the keg was loaded on the next ship out. In London the Company men paid the remains due respect then sent them off to Liverpool for shipment back to Canada. But the keg sat in a storage shed on the Mersey River for nearly two years before it was discovered and shipped to Montreal. True to his wishes, Mr. Rowand's remains were laid to rest in Mount Royal cemetery, but it took them four long years to get there. What's more, when they emptied the keg it wasn't rum that poured out, it was water!"

McMicking laughed, shook his head and said to Brazeau, "Only in this wild land could such a thing happen. Pray that our mortal remains find a resting place more quickly than did Rowand's!"

Later that night, Callihoo gathered together some fellow Indians and half-breeds who sang, beat drums and even did a war dance to entertain the overlanders. Then the overlanders brought out their musical instruments, and played and sang themselves. Such was the extent of everyone's enjoyment that they agreed to have a party again the following night.

It was a more formal affair, with much dancing. Most of the women attending were married and accompanied by their husbands, but that did not prevent the men, at least those whose feet were not skinned and sore from being in water all the time, from having the time of their lives. McMicking was in top form and was determined not to miss a single dance. Once he learned the protocol for acquiring a partner his slate was full, for they found him a handsome man and a skilful dancer. Since none of the women, Catherine excepted, spoke English, all that was required of him was to walk over to one he'd like to dance with, touch her arm, then return to his seat. If she accepted she came to him; they would dance, then return to their respective places without a word passing their lips. And, oh, could they dance! They whirled round the floor in their brightly coloured dresses and soft calf-skin boots with such abandon it all but took his breath away. Flushed with drink, he found the women extraordinarily exotic, and to feel their softness was nothing short of heaven. Their full breasts excited him, and any shame he might have felt was subdued by the blessed release from the rigours of the trail. Best of all, though, was the dance with Catherine Schubert. Considering the number of her potential partners, he was lucky to have a turn, but he had caught her eye and it seemed to be enough. He wanted the evening to go on forever, but it did the next best thing and continued till the early hours of the morning.

Catherine was kept as busy on the dance floor as she had been on the trail. She had felt as worn out as old moccasins just three days ago, and dancing would have been unthinkable. But the time spent waiting for the boats had revived her and she was more than ready for the night's festivities. When she looked around the big room and saw white men dancing with native women and those of mixed blood, and recalled the performance from the night before, she thought herself a long way from Ireland in more ways than one. If there was a down side to the evening at all, it was having only one chance to dance with Thomas McMicking. He was a fine-looking specimen, a gentleman to boot, and no slouch on the dance floor.

On the next day the overlanders got down to the business of buying, selling and trading goods with the half-breeds and Indians for the big push to Cariboo. All their carts were sold, including the democrat wagon, because they wouldn't be practical over the next part of the trail. Instead, the oxen would be used as pack animals, as well as horses, more of which were purchased.

Sellar was miffed. He didn't like any of the transactions, and was convinced the HBC people had the morals of common thieves. They were charging the overlanders $3.50 for saddles that were not worth more than 40¢, and offering only $10, and later $5, for carts that were worth $20 outside the fort. He got so frustrated that he refused to deal with the Company anymore, trading instead with the half-breeds and Indians. Many of the others followed suit, but found the Indians so inconsistent in their understanding of the value of money that it was a trying experience.

Meanwhile, the overlanders were saddened to lose Callihoo's services, and most told him so when they bade him farewell. With his assistance, however, McMicking arranged for a guide to take them as far as Tête Jaune Cache. Callihoo had spoken highly of a man named André Cardinal, and such a recommendation was unassailable. Cardinal was 33 years old, the son of a French fur trader and a Métis woman. He had once been in charge of the

HBC's Jasper House, and apparently had been back and forth between Edmonton and Jasper House 29 times. He had travelled between Jasper and the Cache nearly as many times, and was considered one of the pioneers of the route; no one knew it better than he did. All he wanted for the job was $50, an ox and cart, some flour and some groceries.

There were tales of gold at the fort, big nuggets that lay shining on the sandbars of the North Saskatchewan River. McMicking was accosted by a man who said that he had a claim just a few miles from the fort that produced $15 a day, and was interested in selling it. He had to go away for a while, but upon his return he'd take the colonel there and prove the claim's worth before any money changed hands. McMicking was tempted, but the man failed to show up before it was time for the company to leave. However, no fewer than 25 men said that this was as far as they were going. If there was an Eldorado to be found, they would find it somewhere in this vicinity or they would not find it at all. They watched as the rest packed up to leave and were not the least bit envious of the future awaiting them.

To McMicking's mind, the company's departure from Fort Edmonton was like a circus. While the horses and mules had taken readily to the packs of supplies loaded on them, some of the oxen were being particularly obstinate about it. Though they had been content to pull a cart, they didn't care much for being pack animals and let their owners know straight off. They bucked and kicked and scattered supplies everywhere in a bid not to be loaded. A few even tried to escape, and the owners literally had them by the horns, heels dug into the ground, skidding along until it was no longer possible to hang on. Those watching the antics from the sidelines, which included most of the fort's population, were hugely entertained. Most of the overlanders, though, were embarrassed. They had arrived at the fort with heads held high, the experience of 900 miles behind them, and were leaving like greenhorns.

They were a train now, not of carts but of 140 animals and 125 people. Some of the men, and Catherine, were on horseback while others walked, leading their animals with rawhide ropes. Before long the trail offered up a small sample of what was in store for them. It was muddy from the excessive rain in the area, and nowhere, since leaving Fort Garry, had the mosquitoes and flies been as bad. The insects attacked with such ferocity and in such numbers that all of the animals had to be tied together in single file to prevent them from escaping into the bush. The ten miles up to the Catholic mission at St. Albert, sitting on a rise above Big Lake, were all they could tolerate that first day.

The trail from the mission, though reasonably level, was rough and boggy and twisted through dense stands of poplar and spruce trees that made it difficult to tell if any progress was being made. Everything looked the same, as did the flies and mosquitoes that continued to pester the company. Nevertheless, a good mood prevailed, and there was always Wattie to let them know how many miles had been made. After fording several small streams, they came upon a swift-flowing river. A bridge was needed, but all the good timber was on the far side. A few of the men stripped down and made bundles of their clothes, which they tied on the heads of their oxen. Then they drove the animals into the river and swam them across, hanging onto their tails. The water was ice-cold and the men shook uncontrollably when they came out, but felling the trees and trimming them quickly restored the warmth that the river had stolen. The longest trees were placed side by side, spanning the river, and the shortest ones were placed on top, at right angles. This provided a good, solid bridge capable of withstanding considerable weight, and the green wood lent it flexibility. However, it spooked the animals, and they crossed with great reluctance and fear.

They moved on to the east shore of Lac Ste. Anne, two days down the trail, and camped for the night, the rough trail trying their patience all the way. In the morning, the first day of August, six pack horses had gone missing. Eight men stayed behind to search for them, while the others wound their way around the south shore of the lake, crossing yet another frigid slough, this one a mile and a half wide and three to four feet deep. By midmorning they had reached the HBC post and Catholic mission on the lake's western shore. The post's factor was Colin Fraser, an old-timer in the Northwest who had been brought out as Governor George Simpson's private piper in 1827, and decided to stay. He ultimately proved to be better at business than he was at piping, for Simpson complained that he never seemed to have enough wind to fill his bag.

It gave Catherine much pleasure to find such a large Catholic community out here in the wilderness. The mission boasted the first Catholic church to be built west of Fort Garry, which meant that there was a priest to hear confession. That alone made camping here an unexpected blessing. There were also three nuns who had come from Fort Garry by Red River cart in 1857. Catherine was delighted when they stopped by the campsite to visit with her and the children. They were the first white women she had seen since Fort Garry, and the last she would see for some time.

By contrast, Sellar was not impressed. If anything, he was downright uncomfortable, and if the choice had been his to make, he would not have stopped here. He had always viewed Catholicism with a jaundiced eye. It was too dark and mysterious for his liking, too rife with graven images and Papal lies. And yet he felt sorry for Mrs. Schubert and all the others of her faith duped by those lies. They were merely lambs led astray by these people in their black garb, among whom, he was certain, Satan roamed freely. And those three nuns. They were here for one reason and one reason only, and that was the priest's carnal pleasure.

During the afternoon, just as a party was being dispatched to find out what had happened to the men left behind to find the missing horses, they and the animals arrived safe and sound. That evening a meeting was held with André Cardinal to discuss the state of the trail between Lac Ste. Anne and the Cache.

"The local Indians say it's the road that leads to Hell," Cardinal said, "but it doesn't really lead there. It *is* Hell. Even so, of all the trails going to the mountains, this one's the shortest. It's not as steep as the others, either. The pass through the mountains is dangerous in places but it'll be manageable if we're careful. And you wouldn't want to stray too far from the trail into the forest. Not only are there bears and wolves, you might never find your way out again."

Cardinal was a big, solid man, with a square, rugged face scarred by smallpox. When he had something to say it was usually direct and to the point, and he was an exceptional listener, giving the person speaking to him his undivided attention. It was a quality McMicking liked. Moreover, he was grateful that the guide seemed to be as knowledgeable and reliable as Callihoo.

The next morning, as the company was packing to leave, Bill Morrow got too close to the hind end of a bucking ox and was kicked in the face, as if he hadn't had enough trouble back on the Qu'Appelle River when the cart ran over his head. Nothing was broken, but it knocked him unconscious, split his lip and blackened his eyes. He had to be left behind in the care of the nuns.

As the rest of the overlanders left, Colin Fraser stood at the edge of the village, in full Scottish Highlander regalia, with his bagpipes. He first played "Auld Lang Syne," which dampened many an eye in the company, and then broke into "Sound the Pibroch." The latter was a battle song, and it raised goose bumps on the back of McMicking's neck. He considered the tune entirely appropriate.

Soon the trail began to show signs of its reputation. The ground was boggier, the woods thicker and great tangles of deadfall and underbrush blocked the way. A small group of men, in advance of the main party, chopped and slashed a semblance of a path for the others to follow. Sellar always seemed to be there, tireless in his efforts to clear the way and to build bridges where needed. They came upon a spruce swamp so wide that it was impossible to bypass, so they waded through it, splintering into small groups for the task. All that saved them from disappearing in mud several feet deep was the network of tree roots. If someone got stuck they would have to depend on those coming behind for help because nobody in front could turn back.

McMicking was in the lead and his ox was the first to get stuck. It bellowed and squirmed, a panicked look in its eyes, and try as he might he could not pull the animal free. He could hear other animals bellowing and was shamefully thankful that he wasn't alone with his problems. He had no choice but to unload the animal, which took a Herculean effort. Wading through the mud his legs felt weighted and useless, like trying to run in a nightmare, but once the ox was unpacked it was able to free itself. He reckoned that if he put the same load back on, the frightened creature might never get out of the swamp, so he threw away the heavier items for which he had no use on the trail. Ironically, most of these were mining tools purchased back in St. Paul. He felt foolish doing so, but found out later that most of the company had to do the same thing.

By supper time, they had won 18 difficult miles and everyone, especially those involved in the clearing parties, was exhausted. They camped for the night on the north shore of Lake Isle, a small body of water spotted with tiny islands. Stragglers arrived for hours afterwards, among them Alexander Fortune who had left late from Lac Ste. Anne. Not only did he have to contend with a churned-up swamp, but he was followed by wolves for part of the way. "Providence saw me through," he said, "but there are men who will be laying up for the night back along the trail because they are too tired to reach this campsite."

Providence was not as kind to George Wonnacott, from the Toronto party, who was one of the men bringing up the rear. He had slipped in the bog and hurt his knee so badly that he nearly blacked out from the pain. The weight of his pack and his clothes pushed him under but he was able to grab hold of a root to prevent himself from sinking completely. He clung to the root for the longest time, unable to move because of his knee and the tremendous weight he was bearing. Later, he could hear gunfire from up ahead, and knew it was others in the company trying to give him a bearing to camp, but he was helpless to do anything about it. Time passed. He smeared mud on his face to keep the mosquitoes from devouring him. He eventually realized that nobody was coming back for him and if he didn't do something he would die there. The thought was so terrifying that it gave him the strength to pull himself out hand over hand, root by root, inch by inch. He ignored the pain in his knee; pain was the truth of his existence, the most useful survival tool he had and it helped get him free. Finally, he reached solid ground, scarcely able to move from exhaustion. Then the wolves came.

Fear galvanized him and he arose, a muddy apparition, and limped off in the direction of the rifle shots he'd heard earlier. With every agonizing step he glanced back and could see the wolves keeping pace with him, waiting patiently for any sign of weakness that would make him easy prey. He didn't know how long it took him to reach the other stragglers, but it felt like a lifetime. He panted into their camp looking like a mouldering body just risen from the grave.

The incident profoundly disturbed some of the men. Each wondered what would have happened if he had been back there alone? Would he have found the strength to pull himself free? Maybe, maybe not. Perhaps his last mortal moments would have been fighting for air in a dismal swamp in the middle of nowhere, his only monument a hurriedly scratched letter by someone to a wife or parent, regretting to inform them that their loved one had disappeared somewhere along a trail that had proved to be too much for him to handle.

During the night the stragglers worried about bear attacks, and huddled under their blankets clutching their guns. Then the wolves started up, howling at a gibbous moon, whining and snuffling in the bushes so close it seemed like a single great beast ready to devour them. When they finally fell silent, other sounds from the restless forest were exaggerated in the still night air: owls hooting and small animals stirring, leaves rustling and twigs shifting. And every sound implied a threat. The men hardly slept at all and were up early the next day. Luckily it was the Sabbath and they were able to catch up with the others and enjoy once more the safety found in numbers.

Those up front savoured the luxury of recovering from the previous day's toil and gorging on the soapberries that grew in abundance in the area. They also paid particular attention to their animals, many of which had sore, chafed backs from loads that were improperly tied on. Cardinal spent considerable time showing the men the best way to do it. He scolded a few of them. "Be kind to your animals," he said. "It is what you owe them for the job they are doing."

The last man to arrive in camp that day had stayed behind in Lac Ste. Anne for news from the east and had brought a copy of Toronto's *Globe* newspaper. It was dated May 16, so the news was three months old, but it was the last the overlanders would hear of what was happening in the Canadas and the world until they reached their destination.

McMicking, Sellar and Cardinal set off early Monday morning to lead the way and clear a path for the others. They fought their way through bush and mud for eight terrible miles to the end of Lake Isle, unpacking and repacking their horses nearly a dozen times to free them from the mire. The men were so covered in mud that they were scarcely recognizable as human beings let alone as individuals, but their hard work was rewarded by five miles of comparatively good trail that brought them to the

Pembina River by four in the afternoon. The river was wide, fast-flowing and too dangerous to attempt crossing without help, so they pitched camp to wait for the rest of the company. They would do the crossing in the morning when they were fresher and there were more hands around to make it safer.

The cooking fires that night were fueled by coal taken from huge exposed seams lining the river banks. Those who knew about such things said the quality of the coal was superior to eastern sources. For Catherine, it brought back memories of Ireland, and she was reminded how much she preferred cooking over a coal fire as opposed to wood. The latter might be better for warming up a cold body but the heat from coal was more consistent and less intense.

A pall of dirty grey smoke hung below the top of a nearby hill. After supper, some of the more curious, McMicking included, decided to investigate it. Climbing to the summit, they discovered that the smoke was coming from the ground itself and the soil was hot to the touch. McMicking used his walking stick to dig down a few inches. The earth was so hot he could not leave his hand on it. The air was gaseous and uncomfortably warm, and nothing grew in the vicinity. The ground from which the smoke rose covered a few acres and was slightly depressed so, when asked his opinion, McMicking said that they must be standing in the caldera of a small volcano. It was unsettling, but Cardinal didn't think it was anything to worry about. It had been smoking that way for years.[1]

The overlanders awoke the next morning to icicles hanging from the trees, the sky a wondrous display of stars and planets. They fortified themselves with a good breakfast, then began the task of crossing the Pembina River.

The river was about 70 yards wide and five feet deep, with a good current running. It was cold. They built a raft to ferry the supplies across but it was swept away in the swift water before anything could be piled on it. A search up and down the river for a good ford proved unsuccessful. Cardinal said they would have to use the tents as boats. He had the men spread the tents out flat and pile items damageable by water in the centre. The sides were then drawn up and tied at the top with a short rope for towing. The bundle was carried to the water where two men on horseback towed it across while two other men waded behind to make sure it didn't capsize. Less critical supplies were held in front of a mounted rider. Augustus and two of the strongest riders took the children across, while Catherine ignored offers of assistance and rode the buckskin through the swift-flowing water herself. The horses handled the crossing easily, whereas the oxen panicked and swam in every direction except the one they were supposed to. The crossing went fairly smoothly once a routine was established, but it was noon before the company was able to put the river behind it.

Once more Sellar and a small party went ahead to clear a path. A ravine leading to the top of a bluff gave them a bit of trouble, and beyond that, several demanding creeks and swamps were met and conquered. During the afternoon, in the absence of wind, the sun became stiflingly hot, even among the trees. Everyone's clothes dried out and the chill from the icy river left their bones, but it was merely a short transition from one misery to another. They were soon as soaked in sweat as they had been in river water, and insects by the millions, revived by the heat and offering no quarter, attacked them mercilessly. Flies buzzed maddeningly about, seeking moisture from sweaty faces, and orifices in which to lay their eggs. When the flies weren't attacking, even larger and more predatory swarms of mosquitoes eagerly took their place. The men cursed and swatted at them while the animals noisily complained, shaking their heads, twitching their hides and swishing their tails in a battle only the insects could win.

By late afternoon they had reached the Lobstick River, a tributary of the Pembina, and followed its bank for a while before setting up camp for the night.[2] Their prodigious effort had brought them only 12 miles. Morale was low from the day's heavy slogging, and many men were beginning to wonder if they would be able to keep up the killing pace. McMicking decided that a few rousing fiddle tunes might help set things right. As the music filled the air it was a welcome reminder that the world extended far beyond the boundaries of the campsite, beyond the trackless forest, to civilized places where men in clean clothes sat down with time to compose such rich and complex tunes. McMicking sighed and recalled that Samuel Johnson once wrote that had he learned to play the fiddle he might not have done anything else. It required little effort to understand why.

At first light, the company was able to ford the river to the south side, but there'd been another good frost overnight and not only was the air cold, the water was like ice. Once across, the trail conditions continued to be rough, over swampy ground and through a large blow-down area — a jumble of fallen trees that crisscrossed each other like pick-up sticks. Most were too high to climb over and had to be removed by hand or chopped through. Luckily, the ground was reasonably firm and progress was only slightly hindered. By the end of the day 20 miles had been logged, the best day's travel since they had left Fort

Edmonton. The work was exhausting, but they had done well, and knew pride because of it.

Thursday morning was grey with low clouds and rain, so McMicking treated the company to a couple of hours' extra sleep. Sellar was just as glad. He was feeling miserable from a badly infected finger that had throbbed painfully all night and didn't think he could handle an axe. He had even asked Wattie to take his place in the vanguard.

The trail ran through spruce bogs all day long, the animals at the rear having to struggle through stirred-up mud that was belly-deep. In the late afternoon, they re-crossed the Lobstick to its north bank, and by 6:30 called it a day. They had logged 19 miles, but, because the conditions were worse for those in the rear, people were lagging behind. Many didn't show up in camp that night.

Sellar's finger was still painful the next morning. Worse, he had a boil on his leg and complained of lumbago from the hard work and sleeping on the damp ground. Had these ailments struck him at home they would have been handled easily, but in these circumstances they were brutal and would be a long time healing. He couldn't do a thing without aggravating one or more of his problems, and it was a struggle for him to even get out of bed, never mind make his way across the unforgiving land. For a man whose passion it was to be first away every morning, it was pure torture. In a week and a half he would be 28 years old, but he felt closer to a hundred.

Not far from camp they were confronted with the worst slough so far. It wasn't big, only a half a mile wide, but it almost swallowed them up. At first glance, it looked like mossy ground with small spruce trees blown down and scattered all around, but the moss was merely a façade that hid a bog of floating bark mulch. The men sank to their calves, but the weaker horses and oxen, with their heavy loads, sank up to their necks. Some 15 or 20 were caught this way and all an owner could do was hold his animal's head above the surface till there were enough men available to help pull it out. One ox was stuck so deep and fast that even unloaded, it couldn't be moved. It was put out of its misery by a bullet in its brain. At one point, the entire company was mired in the slough. More unnecessary items were discarded: once again, mostly mining equipment. In the end the men shouldered the goods themselves, including the Schuberts' children, and carried them to firmer ground. One man's horse kicked him in the ankle while they were clambering out of the bog, and the joint was so painful he could barely walk. Later, he accidentally banged it against a tree and the pain disappeared. He figured the horse must have dislocated one of the small bones in his ankle, and the tree knocked it back to position.

It took the company four hours to cross this small stretch of land. When they were finished, they had strained muscles, sore backs and festering blisters. They felt like slaves, and in a sense they were: slaves to the demanding wilderness and their ambition. Had they known before they left, back in April, that it would be like this, few would have made the choice to be here. They forded the Root River that afternoon, and finally called it a day at 6:30, having covered 20 miles.[3]

Sellar was as tough as any man on the trip, but he felt as if he was on his last legs. He had just spent the most miserable day of his life. Every branch or limb that had to be pushed out of the way pained his finger, every press of his pant leg against the boil was excruciating, and he was convinced that because of his back

135

he might never walk straight again. That night he painfully paced the campsite, unable to sit and enjoy the fire with the others, wondering if things could get any worse.

Sellar was not alone in his misery. Others shared similar or worse afflictions, which were now a fact of life on the trail: bruises, boils, carbuncles, fungal infections, insect bites, sprained and swollen joints, skin rubbed raw between thighs, in crotches and armpits, all exacerbated by the relentless hard work, constant cold water and mud baths. Many men had brought their own small supplies of medicine, which disappeared rapidly because of the conditions. Catherine had used up most of hers as well, except some laudanum she kept for the children to help them sleep on difficult nights and some oil of cloves for toothaches. But her Perry Davis Pain Killer and the tincture of leopard's bane that she rubbed on her swollen joints had gone quickly with Augustus and so many others using it. To ease the discomfort of bites, she brewed tea from flowers that grew near the bogs, but it was a losing battle. When she saw Sellar pacing in front of his tent, she went to offer help and he felt miserable enough to tell her his list of ailments. She asked if he'd seen Dr. Stevenson.

"The poor man has enough on his plate already," he replied, "without having to deal with the likes of me. I'll be all right."

Catherine rolled her eyes. "Sure, and didn't I hear the same story from my own husband just this morning, and you couldn't have found a grain of truth in it with a chemist's scale. Nevertheless, you'll be better than 'all right' if you let me deal with that boil. Come with me."

She turned away so abruptly that, before Sellar realized it, he was following her back to her tent like a puppy. It was as if he had suddenly lost any ability to decide for himself whether he should do as she said, and it annoyed him.

"We've got a boil to lance," she told Augustus. "If you'll fetch a clean piece of cloth and soak it in hot water, I'll get a needle. You can sit yourself down, Mr. Sellar, and show that boil to me."

What was there to lose? Sellar lowered himself painfully to the ground. His pants were too tight to roll up, and propriety would not permit shedding them, so he took his knife and made a slit in his pant leg, just above the knee. He could stitch it up later. He exposed the boil, a fiery red pustule as big as a penny. How could something so small hurt so much, he wondered.

"Now, Gus," Catherine said, "if you'll just poke a hot coal from the fire, we'll be done in no time at all."

Once a glowing ember lay outside the fire, she stuck the tip of the needle into it for a moment. Then, gripping Sellar's leg, she pierced the boil twice, near the top, as quickly as she could. Sellar winced in pain and moaned, though he had hoped he wouldn't. The boil erupted like a small volcano and the relief he felt was instantaneous. Catherine squeezed until she was sure most of the poison was gone and Sellar was surprised by the strength in her hand.

"I'll have that hot cloth now, and another dry one, if you please," she said to Augustus, who was wincing himself. She took and carefully folded the hot, damp cloth and pressed it on the sore, then made it secure by tying the dry piece around Sellar's leg.

"This will draw out any poison I missed," she told him. "When the cloth cools, reheat it a couple of times, then once more before you go to bed. Your leg should be right as rain come morning."

Sellar thanked Catherine and, not wanting to be in her debt, insisted on paying for her services. On to his game, she shook her head and smiled.

"Keep your money, Mr. Sellar. Now, if you'll excuse us, there's a long road tomorrow that we'll need to rest up for. Mind what I told you now."

Returning to his tent he felt dismissed, but supposed he deserved it. He had probably insulted her by offering money when she was only trying to help out. He thoroughly disliked being beholden to anybody, especially a woman. Especially a Papist. Apparently she did not understand that there were lines between them, Protestant and Catholic, that should never be crossed. He knew exactly where they were drawn; why didn't she? Why couldn't she just keep to her own kind? He took a pot of water that was hanging over the fire, poured some in a tin cup and made a hot compress. He did it twice more, then went to bed.

Sellar's problems did not prevent the rest of the Huntingdon party from being first up and away in the morning, the first over the fresh ground while it was still reasonably firm. The trail remained boggy, the forest dense and insect ridden. In that desolate stretch of woods, they came upon a small clearing that contained a gravesite, a low mound that was slowly sinking in on its occupant. Carved in a nearby tree was a name, James Doherty, and the date he died, October 1860. Nearly two years ago. It occurred to McMicking that those who buried him were probably not sure of the day, perhaps not even sure of where they were. It was a sobering thought. The thing that disturbed him the most about dying on this journey was to be buried in a place like this, so lonely and remote that it might never be visited by friends and loved ones.

He could see that many of the company were affected by the lonely grave and its simple epitaph. It reminded them of the precariousness of their own circumstances and, more particularly, their own mortality. The impact was profound and momentarily silenced them. They stood there in the shadowy silence beneath the canopy of trees, heads bowed, while Fortune spoke a few words over the grave.

"A brother lies here," he said, his voice resonant and rising. "A man, once like us, of flesh and bones, of sinew and blood, of hopes and dreams. His grave, any grave, reminds us that we are as near to Death as a heartbeat. But there is comfort in the words of David, who said, 'If I take the wings of the morning, and dwell in the uttermost parts of the sea; even there shall thy hand lead me, and thy right hand shall hold me.' God be merciful to our brother's soul, and God save all here."

A murmur of "Amens" rose from the crowd, and on Catherine's face, a single tear slid down, as much for her children, Augustus and herself, as for James Doherty.

Before departing, a couple of men left their own inscriptions on a tree so that passersby might know that others had come this way with greater success than Mr. Doherty. They peeled a patch of bark off a spruce tree and with the burnt end of a stick scratched their names and hometowns in the resin, saying they were on their way to Cariboo. They ended with these understated words: "…a hard road to travel."[4]

They pushed on and reached the McLeod River by mid-afternoon. It was twice as wide as the Pembina, and much colder. Their way across was blocked by a logjam that would have been impossible to get the animals over, so they looked for another ford. A mile or so upstream they found a good one that wasn't so deep that the packs had to be removed to cross it. Nevertheless, the current was substantial and the bottom consisted of slippery cobblestones.

"This is more dangerous than it looks," Cardinal told McMicking. "You'd best warn the company to stay on the backs of their animals, or hang onto their tails, and not try to wade across. The river will have them if they do!"

McMicking had the warning passed back along the column. Catherine's heart was in her mouth, as the mare trod carefully over the treacherous stones. She'd never learned to swim, although a fat lot of good that would have done her in this river. She left the crossing to the mare, trusted the animal's instincts, and both were soon tottering safely up the far bank. Then she watched with apprehension as the children were brought over. One slip and they could be lost to her forever, but they were carried by the best riders on the strongest horses, and were quickly by her side. Then she watched aghast as two men flagrantly ignored the warning and waded into the river. They hadn't reached midstream before they were numb with cold, unable to go any farther, and in immediate danger of being swept away to their deaths. Catherine screamed.

Cardinal turned and assessed the situation in an instant. He spurred his horse into the river, splashing, urging it over the hazardous bottom as quickly as he could without suffering a spill. He shouted at the men to take hold of the horse's tail. In a moment he was upon them, and swung about. Both men grabbed on and Cardinal towed them to shore. By then they were so weakened from the cold that they had to be carried onto dry ground.

Darkness fell before everyone got across the river, so camps were set up on both banks. The location was beautiful, a forest cathedral of arrow-straight, towering spruce trees that were no more than two feet thick at the base, with very little underbrush to speak of. It was like a park; a fine place to spend the Sabbath.

On Monday morning, those who had crossed the river late wanted to stay in camp for an extra day to rest their animals, so the company split up. The lead party followed the twisting ribbon of the McLeod, still through thick forests, up and down hills, and across the rapid streams that joined it. They travelled until one o'clock before they found a place that offered an abundance of grass for the animals. That was when Fortune noticed that his best horse, a cream, had somehow strayed from the caravan, unnoticed, carrying a pack full of supplies. He was thoroughly annoyed with himself for allowing such a thing to happen. Not only did he need the supplies, but in all good conscience he could not leave the horse to fend for itself. He backtracked nearly six miles before he found the animal battling flies amongst the trees. It came to him willingly, and when he rode into camp that night, the cream trailing behind him, the men let out a cheer. Fortune did not feel he deserved it.

The next day passed without incident, along the river, up bluffs and down into gullies, and luckily the ground was firm and dry. That night the rear party arrived in camp, having caught up because they had only taken a half-day's rest back at the McLeod and the trail had been good. The train was whole again and McMicking was glad. Cardinal told everyone that he hoped they had enjoyed the easy day's travel because tomorrow they would be up to their waists again in a spruce bog.

That wasn't exactly news that Catherine wanted to hear, but it seemed as if there was always more bad news than good on this leg of the journey. As she and Gus Jr. were gathering boughs for their beds, she saw Sellar and McMicking talking down by the river. As usual, the Huntingdon man was animated, while the colonel seemed to be listening intently. She wished she could have overheard the conversation, but it was probably something quite ordinary. Sellar could wave his arms while asking for the time of day, and never seemed to have two feet on the ground at the same time. McMicking was just the opposite, as firmly grounded as those giant spruce trees back on the McLeod River. Sure, he could be harsh sometimes, but there were a few men in this company who could bring out the harsh side of a saint. Indeed, Sellar was one of them, with his impatience and intolerance of others. But the colonel always bent over backwards to be fair and he almost always showed good judgment, and for that he had earned and deserved everyone's respect. He was the best man for the job, all right. Wasn't it written all over him from the very start?

Once the children were down she and Augustus had a last cup of tea, and he a last pipe, then before retiring she took what was left in the kettle to the nearest tents and poured cups of the steaming brew for those who wanted some, until it was gone.

True to form, Sellar and the Huntingdon men arose shortly after two o'clock the next morning, wanting to be first to the bog before it was transformed into a sea of mud. Much to their surprise, others had already arisen, hoping to beat them at their own game. It was a close race, but Sellar and his party were too well practised in the art of being away first to be beaten by amateurs.

The bog had burned recently, the trees now pathetic charred sticks, many of them blown down into a snarled mess. Beneath it, the ground was like quicksand, and gripped the animals so tightly the men had to use poles to lever them out. Several hours later they emerged on the far side, crossed the James River, and spent the rest of the morning fording a monotony of streams. Coming out of the trees at noon, they ascended a small rise, and there on the horizon, angular and dark blue, with snow-draped peaks shining in the sun, were the Rocky Mountains. They looked as if the company could almost reach out and touch them.

"You'd have to have a long reach," said Cardinal with a laugh. "About a hundred miles, in fact."

Most of the overlanders were awe-struck. Who among them had ever seen mountains like these before? What they had called "mountains" back home were mere hills compared to these titans. And snow on their tops in summer! They looked formidable yet welcoming, for they seemed to offer an end to the endless spruce bogs and rivers that made up this godforsaken part of the country.

They made good time over dry ground during the afternoon and rejoined the McLeod River, which had dipped south of their course for a dozen miles or so. They crossed yet another burned-out area with a confusion of downed trees. Cardinal called these areas "*brulés.*" When it came time to stop for the night, all the good campsites appeared to be on the far side of the Mcleod, which was too deep and swift to ford at this late hour. As there was no room among the trees to put up the tents, they threw them on the ground and used them as beds. But few slept. They had turned the horses and oxen loose to forage for the night, and the animals wandered through the camp, stepping on people and generally making a nuisance of themselves. The only ones to awaken rested in the morning were the Schubert children who, with the help of the laudanum, were able to sleep through almost anything.

The lack of sleep made travelling difficult the next day. A new trail had to be chopped through the forest as the old one had been washed away during the spring melt; however, now that the river was down, there were beaches that the company could descend to for easier travel. A beaver meadow provided a good lunch stop, and that night camp was set up next to a crystal-clear spring. McMicking had hoped they would reach the Athabaska River that day, but they pulled up to camp well short of it. Still, every step they had taken was a dry one, and that amounted to a good day in anybody's book.

Sellar noticed that one of his mules was bleeding. A pick, poorly stowed in the saddle pack, had worn through and cut into the poor animal's leg with every step. It was wounded so badly there was nothing he could do but lead it into the forest and shoot it.

Cardinal was annoyed. "Unless you are strong enough to carry all your goods yourself," he told Sellar, "you need to pay more attention to the welfare of your animals."

Sellar searched his mind for an excuse but couldn't find one. He alone was responsible. He would have to be more careful from now on, not only for his animals' sake, but for his own. However, he didn't like being dressed down by a half-breed, even if he deserved it.

The mountains loomed closer with every mile as the trail climbed and descended over one hill after another, the ground so rough and rocky that there was no feed for the animals. The only consolation was that they were in the foothills now. At last they reached the Athabaska, its waters sparkling and pristine, the most beautiful river they had seen so far. They followed its south bank deeper into the foothills, fording tributaries, crossing sloughs and slashing their way through heavy underbrush in the forest. All the while, the landscape rose and fell above the river. Oh, McMicking fantasized, if that river were but a macadam highway, how easy their lot would be! Then the trail veered to the southwest and the river disappeared from view. They camped on the bank of Maskuta Creek, a mountain-fresh tributary of the Athabaska, and drank water so cold it made their teeth ache.[5] Cardinal told them that before swallowing it they should hold the water in their mouths to warm it up.

"You've built up a lot of body heat," he explained, "and you'll probably get a bad case of stomach cramps otherwise."

On Sunday, part of the company wanted to move on. There was a sense of urgency to get where they were going, to get into the mountains and beyond them. Not only were their supplies getting low but there had been precious little feed for the animals, which were now having to forage so far afield at night that considerable time was spent in the morning trying to round them up. And even though it was only the middle of August, the nights were distinctly cooler and Cardinal kept saying the trail ahead was still rough and long. Thus, a day sitting around idle was a day wasted, a day that might place them in jeopardy somewhere down the line.

But just as many didn't want to move, and Fortune argued their case. Rest was needed precisely *because* the way ahead was rough and long. "Have faith in Providence," he said. "It is God's grace that has brought us this far, and God's grace will see us through!"

McMicking called for a vote, and the majority sided with Fortune. They were tired and wanted to stay put and rest. That evening, during the religious service, Fortune reinforced his point by reading from the Psalms: "The ungodly are…like the chaff which the wind driveth away. …The Lord knoweth the way of the righteous: but the way of the ungodly shall perish. … Preserve me O God: for in thee do I put my trust." He couldn't put it any plainer than that.

Sellar, a contradiction of emotions with his restlessness and piousness, was unsettled and slightly depressed. He wanted fervently to be on the move, to conquer those mountains, but everyone in his party had voted to stay. After breakfast he tried his hand at fishing but caught nothing. It only depressed him more. The day seemed to drag on forever, and his mood was fed by loneliness. He needed the comfort of his wife, and since these were things men rarely spoke of amongst themselves, he turned to his diary and wrote her a poem.

> When we two parted in silence and tears,
> Half broken-hearted to sever for years,
> Pale grew thy cheek and cold, colder thy kiss,
> How true that moment foretold trials like this.[6]

Catherine watched Sellar writing in his diary. She didn't quite know what to make of the man. He was so driven to make progress that he didn't care whose toes he stepped on. No, that's not quite fair. More accurately, he didn't *think* about whose toes he stepped on. He didn't think much of Catholics, either; she could feel that from him. Even though he always treated her with respect, she easily sensed the wide space he put between them; lancing his boil had only closed the space a bit. It's a sorrowful thing, she thought, when one person's beliefs are held so much in contempt by another, for the end result is always bigotry. Thank goodness men like Sellar were a minority, for she had had more than her fill of his kind in Ireland.

But for now, Sellar was the least of her worries. Her children were her main concern. The company had left Edmonton nearly three weeks ago and food supplies were running low. Their situation wasn't critical just yet, but it was worrisome. She upset herself thinking that perhaps starvation would be the end of them all before this journey was done. And wasn't the threat of that the reason her family had left Ireland in the first place? Now her own children were faced with the same peril and she alone had led the little dears right to it, like lambs to the slaughter. Later, in bed, she spoke with Augustus about her fears.

"Nothing will happen to the children," he said, drawing her to him. "We'll all see this journey through to its end." And there, in the warmth of his arms, it suddenly became an easy thing to believe.

Had he been completely honest with himself, McMicking would have said that he was more than a little concerned with the decision not to keep moving. He, the man who at the onset of this trek insisted on strict adherence to the Sabbath rule, was now having doubts about it, at least in this particular instance. Every day the trail seemed to get worse instead of better, harder instead of easier. But the majority of the company had voted to stay and stay they would. Though he would have defended to his death the democratic process, he considered it quite onerous at times. One couldn't always depend on the majority to choose wisely, and they might yet suffer the consequences of what he was beginning to think was a poor decision. Nevertheless, it was done. He turned in for the night, longing for the modest civilization he knew existed beyond those treacherous-looking peaks, longing for the lovely familiarity, predictability and the safety of the mundane. It was some time before he drifted off to sleep, his mind as jumbled as trees in a *brulé*. One thought stood out above the rest, though: Were faith and piety really the same thing, as Fortune would have everyone believe?

The company arose at 2:20 the following morning. With feed so scarce and campsites limited, most of the parties were vying for that coveted lead position. They followed Maskuta Creek to the Athabaska, crossing several icy streams along the way, truly among the mountains now, and stopped to camp for the night beneath the long shadow of Roche Miette, its monolithic top towering above them. On the north side of the river were other equally stunning mountains that were almost frightening in their beauty. It was as if they were surrounded by the very crown of the world.

The air was thick and heavy, the sky ominous, and shortly after nightfall there were blinding flashes of lightning, one after the other, like daguerreotype cameras going off in sequence. These were followed immediately by tremendous explosions of thunder that bounced back and forth off the mountain walls before dissipating in the ether. Thick clouds drifted across the campsite and enveloped it, and when the lightning wasn't flashing, the night was as black as jet. This was nothing like the electrical storms on the prairies or back in the Canadas, where they seemed to always be above you. Here, among the mountains, it was more like being right *inside* them. It was nature in its most spectacular form, and it was terrifying. Catherine had never felt so disoriented and vulnerable. It was easy to believe that those stupendous lightning bolts and explosions of thunder would rend the mountains apart and bring them tumbling down upon their heads. Would she and her family go to sleep this night never to wake up again, their resting-place for eternity beneath an avalanche of stone? She prayed that it wouldn't be so, she prayed until the thunder was a far-off rumble and the night became silent. And still she couldn't fall asleep.

The next morning the company had gone only a mile up the Athabaska when Cardinal called a halt. "There is an important decision to make," he told McMicking. "You'd best call a meeting." Once the company had assembled he laid out what he knew of the trail ahead.

"From here," he said, "we have a choice of two routes and both of them are dangerous." He explained that they could cross to the north side of the river, which was something they would have to do sooner or later, but doing it here meant that they would be faced with two wide tributaries that were swift and glacial. These would have to be followed upstream for a considerable distance in order to find a suitable fording spot, and that wouldn't be easy. The alternative entailed staying on the south side of the river, and crossing further upstream. There was only one tributary that could be forded easily, but beyond it was a mountainside that had to be partially climbed and skirted. The path was narrow and the footing treacherous, and the animals wouldn't like it a bit, never mind their owners.

"Which way do you think we ought to take?" someone asked.

"Well, one's as bad as the other, but I suppose it comes down to what scares you most: water or heights. I'm not partial to either, but if you want to get where you're going, you do whatever it takes. At any rate, the decision is yours to make, not mine."

McMicking knew which route he preferred, but it was the kind of decision that required a vote. He could tell by the uproar of voices that whichever route won out it wouldn't be by a large margin. A show of hands was asked for, first for the mountain, then for the river. The mountain won by a slim majority. He suspected that there were probably a few on the losing side who feared that the democratic process had just decided their manner of death, but he himself was relieved. The fewer river crossings he had to make, the better he liked it.

After fording the tributary they rounded a nub of land that Cardinal called Disaster Point, then began the climb up the mountainside, leading the pack animal, and letting the riderless saddle horses follow along. It was seven in the morning. The weather was dull, but at least it wasn't raining. The pitch was steep and they had to bend into it, climbing slowly to allow the animals sure footing. Up they went, panting and sweating, straining leg muscles they hadn't yet used, along a path that seemed as narrow as a tightrope. Above them, to their left, were myriad goat tracks and the cube of Roche Miette against a backdrop of thick cirrus clouds. To their right was a steep drop to the Athabaska River which looked more and more like a small stream with every step they took. Farther up the valley they could see Jasper Lake, a huge, dark mirror reflecting the mountains around it. On the opposite side of the river was Jasper House, an HBC post that Cardinal said was unoccupied, so there was no point in going there.[7] From where the overlanders stood it didn't look much bigger than a chicken coop.

A swarm of hornets came out of nowhere and attacked them. There was no escaping the stinging insects and they panicked some of the animals. One of the horses lost its footing when it tried to turn around and go back. It tumbled over the side, clattering down amongst the sliding detritus for more than a hundred feet, its eyes wide with terror, before being caught in some stunted trees at the edge of a cliff. Beyond that was a vertical drop of nearly a thousand feet. Catherine's heart was in her mouth. (It was the only time she dared look down, and it almost made her swoon.) The horses were precious to them, not only for the work they did, but also because of the attachments so easily formed between humans and animals. The bright side was that it was a saddle horse rather than a pack horse, so no provisions were lost, and the poor creature appeared to be all right. It was struggling to get back on its feet as two men slid down to rescue it. Another stood by ready to shoot it should that prove necessary. Amazingly, the animal escaped with only a few superficial scratches.

They reached an altitude of 1,700 feet above the river before the trail began to descend. It dropped steeply into a saddle at first, then rose again before sloping more gently down to the river. The path twisted, and was so narrow that the packs of the horses rubbed against the cliff face beside them. The view ahead of the saw-tooth peaks of the Jacques Range was stunning and provided a temporary diversion for those afraid of heights. The descent was harder on their calf muscles than the ascent had been, and by the time they had reached the valley bottom many of the men were wobbly and barely able to stand. Catherine could have kissed the earth beneath her feet, so relieved was she to be off that slender ledge. She felt giddy, caught somewhere between laughter and tears, and had to sit down.

Their course was now that of the river. They followed it assiduously, climbing and descending, again and again, sometimes wading through ice-cold water more than three feet deep. They stopped for lunch amid wildflowers on a sliver of land between Jasper and Talbot lakes, the mountains soaring around them. Afterward, they followed the beach, gravelly and hard on the animals' hooves, then climbed a couple of hundred feet to a rocky bench, before dropping down on the far side. Another mile and a half and they pulled up for the night.

What an unbelievable day it had been! They had traversed what seemed to some like the top of the world, and covered 18 miles to boot. They were immensely pleased with themselves. What's more, there was, at last, ample pasturage, so the animals could feed to their hearts' content. And that was the real icing on the cake.

They would need that confidence, and more, Cardinal knew, to get them through the coming days. "I hope they sleep well," he told McMicking. "They'll need it because tomorrow's road will make today's seem like a picnic."

The morning saw them another mile and a half upstream, having climbed and descended yet another point of land. This was where they would cross the Athabaska, where it was deep and wide, and the current not as strong as it was in narrower channels. There was an abundance of fellable trees near the shoreline and the company set about building several rafts for the crossing. The largest one measured eighteen feet long by eight feet wide, and they were able to get all their goods over in four trips. Then they swam the animals across, Fortune's cream horse leading the way. Those that were reluctant to enter the deep water were led over from the rafts. The crossing went smoothly, but it took the entire morning.

The caravan then started up the broad valley, which was plugged with deadfall. They hacked their way through — a yard, a rod, a furlong — raised new blisters on old ones, and sweated off even more pounds. They put ten hard-won miles behind them and called it a day. There was music in camp that night, slow and mellow, as everyone wanted it, and it soothed their tired minds and aching bodies.

The temperature plunged below freezing overnight, so everyone slept in till 5:30. A short distance farther up the valley they entered the gorge of the Miette River, which would take them up to the Continental Divide. It wasn't far, a couple of dozen miles, but even Cardinal had no idea how difficult it would be, how much it had changed since the last time he was through.

As they made their way up the narrow gorge, the first few miles were deceptively easy. Then they encountered the worst *brulé* they had seen thus far. Not only were the downed trees strewn every which way, they were bigger and thicker than in previous *brulés*, and in places stacked ten feet deep. There was no way over, under or around them. Ten men hauled out their axes, and began the chore of clearing a path for the rest of the company. They worked in shifts so that the choppers were always fresh. Axes flew, the dull thud of metal on wood rising above the noisy rush of the river. So many trees had to be cleared away that progress was no longer measured in miles or even yards: it was measured in feet. When a patch of trees was cleared, the ground beneath was usually badly broken and the footing precarious, which hindered progress even more. In the short span of two hours they crossed and re-crossed the Miette seven times, wading through bone-numbing water on slippery stones that threatened to send them cascading downstream. By day's end, they still hadn't reached a place with enough feed for the animals, but they were dead tired and set up camp anyway.

After supper, an argument broke out between Bob Gilbert, a Queenston man, and Joe White, from Huntingdon. There had never been much love lost between the two men, and they had been at each other's throats all day. The bickering went on for some time, each man accusing the other of not pulling his weight.

The recriminations dissolved into name calling, and soon they were standing nose to nose. Gilbert pushed White, who stumbled backwards but never lost his footing. White was filled with rage and he tore into the Queenston man with a flurry of fists. They were the blows of an inexperienced fighter, and Gilbert was able to fend off most of them. He landed a solid punch on White's jaw that momentarily stunned him. Blood seeped from the corner of White's mouth. Then Gilbert lunged at his opponent's chest, and the two went crashing to the ground. They rolled around for several minutes, throwing ineffectual punches at each other, and slowly fatigue began to overtake them. Finally, Gilbert prevailed, having White in a headlock from which he was too tired to escape. They lay like that for a long time, panting, unable to speak. No one in the company stepped forward to break them up, not even McMicking who was both excited and appalled by the entire episode. Gilbert let the Huntingdon man go and stood up. Neither man spoke. There was complete silence in the camp, except for the rushing river and the occasional rumble of rolling rocks in the mountains high above them. White walked away, and went to his tent. Gilbert stayed rooted where he was, watching White leave, then he too collected himself and followed suit.

Have I gone completely mad, McMicking wondered? Why didn't I stop the fight? Or why didn't someone else step in to end it? Even Mrs. Schubert had seemed mesmerized by the whole affair, which disappointed him. One word from her and any number of men would have jumped in. Perhaps we've all gone mad, or are simply too bone-weary to care anymore.

He went to bed, disturbed by his and everyone else's inaction, and resolved that he would not allow such a thing to happen again. All we have out here in this wilderness to show that we are civilized beings, he reflected, is the way we treat each other. If we lose that, then what hope do we have?

Catherine retired equally disturbed. She had sat there gaping like a fool and now felt like one. Why she hadn't said anything she did not know, for words had never eluded her. Perhaps it was because the fight was just waiting for a time and place to happen, and stopping it would have only been putting off the inevitable. It was hard to know. One thing she did know for certain, though, was that it was like a knife cut across the face. The cut might heal but your face would never be the same again.

People were quieter than usual the next morning; the camp was aroused early so that they could push on in hopes of finding feed for the animals. The axemen set off first to clear a path, and the company slowly worked its way upstream, last night's fight all but forgotten in the gruelling, consuming toil of the day. Fortune's favourite ox slid into the river and decided it was easier to get out on the far bank, leaving the Huntingdon man no choice but to strip and swim the frigid water himself to fetch it. He thought he would perish from the cold in the attempt. Later, several pack animals lost their footing and plunged in. They had to be roped and pulled out, but none were hurt and no supplies were lost. The company crossed the Miette once more and pushed through the dense woods along the south bank where the trail was easier for a while. During the afternoon, they came to a flat-topped ridge of land where the valley of the Miette curved away to the river's source in the northwest. The ridge was the Leather Pass, Cardinal told them.[8] From now on the rivers would flow with them rather than against them. They had reached the Continental Divide.

It should have been a momentous occasion, but no one was in a celebratory mood. They drove on a couple of comparatively easy miles through the pass, their bowels rumbling like distant thunder from the mineral-rich waters of the Miette, then picked their way slowly along the wooded north shores of Yellowhead and Lucerne lakes, their waters dark blue and rippled.[9] Upon reaching the far end, they pitched their tents for the night.

The sun hid early in these mountains. Dusk was expanded and the surrounding peaks seemed to stand out more boldly against the sky, as if to defy the coming shroud of night. High above the camp were the forested shoulders and rugged crest of Yellowhead Mountain. Far across the thickly wooded valley, dominating the southeastern sky, was the barren peak of Mount Fitzwilliam, streaked with snow. Both mountains were nameless to the overlanders. A pair of eagles screeched overhead as if admonishing these humans for invading their territory, and a wolf pack began howling farther down the valley.

The company had crossed the divide in more ways than one. Food supplies were critically low now, not only for themselves but also for the animals, which were even worse off. There had been such an abundance of feed for them between Forts Garry and Edmonton that they had actually put on weight during the trip. However, since leaving Fort Edmonton, conditions had deteriorated with each passing day and the animals had become gaunt to the point that their rib cages showed badly and many were getting too weak to travel. Two oxen had already been shot and eaten.

As for themselves, the overlanders had originally believed that they would only be on the road two months. Here it was three, and they still had a long stretch to go. They had cut their own rations in half which, combined with the incredibly hard work they were doing daily, was taking its toll on just about everybody. On this night, they had eaten the last of their pemmican, and had to slaughter another ox to replace it. They hadn't enough salt to cure the meat, and had to jerk it instead, a relatively simple process whereby the meat was cut into long, thin strips and dried over a smoky fire. The end result was as tough as old boot leather and about as tasty, but it was a good source of nourishment. Jerking's biggest drawback was that the process was time-consuming.

Catherine still fretted about the children, and always made sure they were fed first. So far they were doing just fine and weren't complaining too much. She knew also that many of the men would not see them go hungry. Even Jim Sellar stopped by, and handed Catherine a package wrapped in rawhide. "It's for the little ones," he said. "I won't be needing it." He walked off before Catherine could say anything. She unwrapped the package and inside was, in all likelihood, the last of Sellar's pemmican. She could have wept.

Crawling beneath his blankets for the night Sellar took stock of his health. The infection on his finger was clearing up, and the boil on his leg was completely gone, thanks to Mrs. Schubert. His back still bothered him, but it was at least tolerable now. Generally, he was feeling pretty good considering where he was and what he'd gone through to get here. But today was his 28th birthday and he would much rather have been celebrating at home, with his family, around a proper dinner table bearing proper food. Instead, he was here among these appalling mountains, drying meat in the manner of savages. Some birthday party this was. Still, he had to admit that giving that package to Mrs. Schubert had helped his disposition no end. Now they were even.

The choppers were away first in the morning and the rest followed later, down along a small creek that soon joined the Fraser River which flowed out of the mountains from the southeast. But the route along the Fraser was rough and excruciatingly slow. They bullied their way through the thick evergreens, enormous tangles of bushes and a number of sloughs, until they had gone seven miles. After lunch they pushed forward another seven that seemed virtually indistinguishable from the last. They had hoped to reach Moose Lake, into which the Fraser flowed, but fell short of their goal by a couple of miles. They camped instead on a hard bed of gravel next to the Moose River, a large tributary where, again, there was no feed for the animals. Once more they had to be satisfied with nibbling on bushes and trees to sustain themselves.

The next day was Sunday, and there was enough desperation in the overlanders' circumstances that, this time, no one argued against moving on to where conditions were better for man and beast alike. They wound their way down the Fraser to where it became a small lake about a mile long and half mile wide. It wasn't deep so they waded in and, despite the relatively warm air in the valley, their legs were numb with cold by the time they were through it. The Fraser narrowed back to a river for only a short distance before it became Moose Lake, a slender body of water stretching ten miles down the valley, with steep mountainsides forming much of its banks. The interminable shoreline was rugged with boulders and gravel that tore painfully at the animals' hooves, and they had to be prodded over the cruel surface, sometimes with more force than the men liked. But caution also had to be exercised for it was prime territory for breaking a leg. One of the Schuberts' pack horses tried to escape the misery by leaping into the frigid water. Augustus went in after it and led the recalcitrant animal back to the jumble of rocks and boulders.

"Do you think there's an end to this lake somewhere in our future?" he asked Catherine, who herself was beginning to wonder.

In some places, a precipitous bank or a rocky outcrop blocked their path, and the only way around was to take to the water. They could find no place to stop and eat. By late afternoon it had become a test of endurance, and Catherine was looking for the end of the lake with every step. When it finally came into view, the slow, painful journey went on till well into the evening before they finally reached it, as worn out by their efforts as they had ever been.

The area did not offer a very good campsite. There was no food for the animals, and the tents would have to be pitched on hard gravel, but the company could go no farther this day.

"Right about now," Sellar groaned, "I might be persuaded to trade my soul to the Devil in exchange for one night in a feather bed."

Others said they would not need to be persuaded and would, in fact, leap at such an offer.

Fortune had just sat down to rest when someone yelled at him to bring his gun. A porcupine had been trapped in a small hole and it would make a fine meal. McMicking was going to join in, but he spotted a skunk. He shot its head off. He skinned the animal, while Fortune and the others burned the quills off the porcupine. The animals were cut into pieces that were stuck on the ends of sticks and roasted over the fire. McMicking wondered why he hadn't tried skunk sooner. Even though there was a hint of the animal's potent smell in the taste of its meat, when covered liberally with the sauce of hunger, it was quite palatable. Indeed, not a single complaint was raised from those with whom he shared the repast.

They needed to get the animals to a feeding place, and that was the company's main concern when they set out Monday morning. Back on the Fraser, they chopped their way down the river to a place where it made an abrupt turn to the southwest and the valley broadened. There was plenty of pasturage here so the overlanders paused for lunch and let the animals eat their fill. The valley was replete with huckleberries as big as grapes, and it offered up a few porcupines as well. The berries in particular were welcome, for a couple of the men were suffering from bleeding gums, one of the first signs of scurvy.

Farther down the river, the valley narrowed, and during the late afternoon, when they searched for a decent campsite, they couldn't find one. They had to make do on the steep mountainside. They wrapped themselves up in blankets and slept where they could stretch their tired bodies out. Some created a flat space for themselves by building tiers from the rocks, while others simply lodged themselves against boulders and trees to keep from rolling down the mountainside. The animals were left to browse for what they could find and wandered through the makeshift campsite all night. Mount Robson loomed above them in the clear night, its snow-laden peak ghostly white against a backdrop of glittering stars.

Even Cardinal was impressed. Of the many times he'd been through the valley he'd never once seen the top of the peak — a shroud of clouds always hid it. But then this route was always changing from one season to the next, and one year to the next. The only thing that was ever the same was the abuse it heaped on the human body and spirit.

Catherine was miserable. She imagined herself luxuriating in a hip bath, like the kind she'd seen in the fancy homes she had worked in as a domestic servant back in Massachusetts, but it only made the reality of her situation worse. She had always been a tireless worker, but this was more demanding than anything she'd ever done. She worried about her unborn child, worried that the stress and strain, day in and day out might cause her to lose it. Yet despite her worries she always made time to help others — a poultice here, a soothing tea there — and those who had voted against her joining the expedition wondered what on earth had ever possessed them to do so. Thomas McMicking, God bless him for the man that he was, always asked how she was doing and once jokingly berated her for doing too much.

"You're shaming the men, Mrs. Schubert," he had said, to which she smiled and replied, "Some are in desperate need of it, Colonel."

The next day the valley sides were cut with glacial rivers and creeks. They cascaded into the valley in waterfalls several hundred feet high, adding themselves to the swelling Fraser River which grew wider, deeper and more powerful with each mile it rushed toward the sea. The valley turned into a gorge and the hillside was treacherous. Several times animals fell and slid 50 feet or more down the slope before they were able to recover. At nine o'clock the company was brought to a halt by a broad talus slope. There wasn't even a semblance of a path across it. With no obvious alternative presenting itself, the men took their picks and shovels and began carving their own trail out of the scree. Four hours later it was wide enough to get the animals across, but without the packs; the men had to carry the supplies across the mountain face themselves. The work left them breathless, for a small slip would mean certain death. Several trips were required to move the supplies from one side to the other, then they had to go back and lead the animals across. One horse panicked on the treacherous path and as everyone watched horrified, it plummeted to its death in the river far below.

By supper time they had reached the spot where the Fraser entered the broad Robson Valley and they pitched their tents for the night. Some crows landed nearby, looking for a scrap of food, only to become food themselves. They were lice-ridden, but once plucked, made a skimpy meal, supplementing the half-rations of some of the campers. The evening was spent talking of home and the fine meals that had been eaten there, the men smoking their pipes to quell their appetites. Then a storm crept into the valley and it rained fiercely.

The camp was awakened the next morning by a cry of "Hurrah for Tête Jaune Cache!" It was Cardinal shouting, and people tumbled out of their tents into the chilly air. He had been up early, out scouting the trail. "If all goes well," he announced, "we should be in Tête Jaune Cache this afternoon!"

It was wonderful news, a magical potion that brought smiles to downcast faces, and energy to weary, sore muscles. Thus refreshed, the company was under way as quickly as possible.

The ups and downs of the landscape were not the trial they had been in previous days; even the bushwhacking seemed easier, and there was much good-natured bantering among the company. Then one of the oxen inexplicably charged over the bank of the river and was swept away in the torrent, pack and all. It was almost as if the animal had grown tired of life as a beast of burden and decided to end it. The carcass was found washed up on a sandbar a mile downstream, minus its load, which was never found.

At 4:30 in the afternoon they reached the place they had sought as avidly as they had sought Fort Garry and Fort Edmonton, a goal that had extracted more from humans and beasts than the other two combined. Yet they had made it. All were much slimmer than when they started out, some suffering greatly, but they had made it. And they hadn't lost a soul. Unfortunately, the treacherous mountains had claimed no fewer than 17 of their animals.

And what was this place that was as much anticipated as those great forts of the plains? Was it a structure equally impressive in size that would once more provide a link, however remote, to the civilization they once knew? A place that hummed with commerce, where men and women dressed up on a Saturday night and danced their cares away, then attended church on Sundays? Or a small post, perhaps, from which mail could at least be sent home to loved ones? No. It was none of these. Tête Jaune Cache, when the overlanders arrived, consisted of two or three teepees and a small band of Shuswap Indians with their dogs on the south shore of the Fraser River, and nothing more.[10] It was simply an anteroom to the rest of British Columbia, a place in which they could catch their collective breath after the rigours of the Divide. But oh, what a thrill it was to be here!

The Robson Valley, in which Tête Jaune Cache was situated, was wide and beautiful, a place of rivers, fall-coloured trees and lush green grass. Woodsmoke hung above the Indian encampment, from smouldering fires above which were racks of salmon being preserved for the coming winter. It was a land of plenty for those who knew how to tap its natural resources, as the Shuswaps did. But for the overlanders, its main resources were the rich grass for the animals to graze on, the trees for building rafts and canoes and the Indians themselves. Each group had things the other wanted and they were soon bartering. In exchange for ammunition, clothes, handkerchiefs, needles and thread, the company got dried salmon, berry cakes and huckleberry wine. In the early evening, several more Indians arrived, with ten freshly caught salmon averaging about 50 pounds each. They soon belonged to the overlanders, the Indians taking just about any usable material item they could lay their hands on. The most popular items were needles and thread.

The irony of these transactions did not escape McMicking. The single biggest fear of the overlanders so far on this journey had been that of being attacked by Indians. Now, in this isolated spot deep among the thick-timbered mountains, where they had been pushed to the very limits of their abilities to cope and survive, the Indians were as good as saviours.

Cardinal asked them about the best route to Cariboo, but it was not a place they had ever heard of. They themselves had come overland from the Shuswap country far to the south, having lost several of their band in an avalanche along the way.[11] It was their opinion that the best route to the lands west of the Cache was south along the North Thompson River, even though it was not a route they knew well enough to offer themselves as guides, or even to give advice about the trail. The one thing they knew for certain was that the Fraser River was probably best avoided. It might look peaceful here but it grew furious farther down, smashing itself into foam, in narrow rocky gorges.

The overlanders had hoped for more details, so the lack of information was disheartening. To make matters worse, it now seemed that whatever they decided to do, they might be doing it without a guide. Cardinal had said back at Fort Edmonton that if an Indian guide could be found at the Cache to take them through to Cariboo, he would go along as an interpreter, but if one couldn't be found he would go no farther. The routes beyond the Cache were unfamiliar to him. So far a guide had not been found, which meant the company would have to find its own way from this point forward.

At a lengthy meeting the possibilities were discussed. There appeared to be three. First, they could go due west and cross overland to Cariboo, through the Premier Range, but even though the distance wasn't more than a hundred miles there was no clear trail, and no one to lead the way. It would be easy to get lost among those mountains, particularly if the weather worsened, as it most surely would. Second, they could go south to the North Thompson River and follow it to Fort Kamloops, then west to the Fraser and north to Cariboo. Though the route was deemed to be easier, it was much longer, at least 500 miles, 200 of them through uncharted territory to the fort. The third possibility was the Fraser River, which ran many miles northwest before it swung south to Fort George and Quesnellemouth, the western gateway to the goldfields. That distance was approximately 300 miles. The Fraser was probably the fastest route but, according to the Indians, it was fraught with danger. Whatever the company decided, it needed to be done quickly; it wouldn't be long before winter began to assert itself. As Cardinal had said, the time between summer and winter in this valley could sometimes be measured with a stopwatch.

After much discussion, and more opinions than there were people, a decision was reached. The bulk of them would build rafts and canoes and try their luck with the Fraser. Since too many rafts would be needed to accommodate all the animals, only a few would be taken to use as food along the way. The rest would be taken over the North Thompson River route to Fort Kamloops by a second, smaller party. The animals would be sold or traded there for whatever could be obtained for them. Then the party would make its way by more conventional routes to Cariboo. Their minds made up, the overlanders began preparing for their departure.

To get suitable timber for the river craft the men had to go up the Fraser four miles. Even those who belonged to the North Thompson party pitched in and helped. There weren't enough tools to go around so the men worked in two shifts, half in the morning, the other half in the afternoon. They chose the straightest trees and the rafts they built were huge — 40 feet long and 20 feet wide, with cross-pieces every few feet. They also fashioned several dugout canoes from cottonwood trees, a few 30 feet long, and lashed them together in pairs for added stability. Meanwhile, those who weren't working on the rafts were busy jerking meat for their respective journeys. Everyone worked at a feverish pace from Thursday through the weekend, even on the Sabbath, and by late Monday afternoon the two parties were ready to go their separate ways.

Sellar and a few of the Huntingdon men had decided to go with the North Thompson party until an old hunter arrived in camp one night and made them rethink their decision. He said that unlike the Fraser route, which was a journey of only days if one survived it, the North Thompson route might take weeks and they would be hard pressed to make it to Fort Kamloops before the snow flew. Upon hearing this vital piece of information Sellar and his friends switched to the Fraser party. The last thing any of them wanted was a few more weeks in this dreadful wilderness. Besides, Sellar, at least, had never been afraid of the water; during the past few weeks, it had almost been his home. So he and the others set to building their own rafts, falling some beautiful cedar trees, and using axes as wedges along the grain to split off perfectly formed boards. From these they built a raft 45 feet long. They put together another from fir and spruce 50 feet long, chinked with slender poles so that the animals it carried wouldn't get their feet caught in the cracks.

McMicking experienced a deep sense of loss at this parting of the ways. Considering the dangers that awaited them on both trails, there was a good chance he would never see many of his companions again. He had grown to admire some of the men taking the North Thompson route, and if he ever had to make a journey like this again — heaven forbid! — then he would gladly have them by his side. Possibly even Sellar.

He held a special place in his heart for Catherine Schubert, who, like only a handful of the men, had made this trip uncomplainingly, pitching in to help whenever her children weren't in need of her attention, and in some instances even setting an example for a few of the others. His thoughts drifted back to the meeting at Long Lake when he had had doubts about bringing a woman along, and he was glad he'd reconsidered his position. In retrospect it was a sound decision that had only benefited the company. Now, it seemed, she was with child again, although it was not common knowledge among the men. Had he known of her condition at the outset, he would never have allowed her to come, and yet here she was, more than a thousand miles of prairie behind her, not to mention the daunting wall of mountains they had just crossed, unscathed and in better shape than many of the men. Though he wished she had been more forthright about her condition, he could certainly understand why she hadn't been. She was a woman of great courage, a woman to admire, no doubt about it. His feelings for her were bound up in pride and gratitude.

He and the Fraser River party would be away at first light tomorrow, so he reckoned he'd best say his goodbyes. He walked over to the Schubert tent. Catherine had just put the children down, brewed a pot of rose-hip tea, and joined Augustus in front of the fire while he had his last pipe of the day. They invited McMicking to sit down, and offered tea.

He declined the tea but sat, removing his hat and placing it on his knee. "It's been a journey," he said.

"Aye," said Catherine. " And it's not over yet."

"No, but it soon will be, and I expect you'll be as happy as I when it's behind us."

"Happier still in a home, which is a far better place to be. We only need to find one."

Augustus smiled. "We'll find one," he said. "But think of it, Catherine. No matter where we are, the distance from heaven is always the same."

" 'Tis true," said Catherine. "But if I'm going to travel there I'd just as soon depart in my old age and from the comfort of a feather bed."

McMicking chuckled. He didn't know quite what to say to this remarkable woman. It would only embarrass her if he said how much he valued her presence, that he, personally, would miss her, and that the Fraser River party would be wanting without her. He might also embarrass himself, for if the truth were known he felt strangely close to tears. Perhaps it was the strain of the past few days and the frightful possibilities of tomorrow, and because he felt responsible for everything, even for the people who would no longer be in his charge. So all he said was, "I'm pleased that you have chosen the North Thompson route. It may be longer, but it should be much safer for you and the children."

It was the truth of what was inside him. It would have been more than he could bear if either she or any of her children had been lost on the river. In a while he rose to leave but didn't really want to. Leaving meant acknowledging that the day had ended and that tomorrow would take its place. And it was tomorrow that he dreaded most, the river, and that he might never see this woman again.

"I wish you both a safe journey," he said.

He shook Augustus' hand, and looked at Catherine. Her eyes shone in the firelight with a film of tears, but her voice was firm. "You're a fine man, Thomas McMicking, and there's no lie in that. God be with you on every road you travel."

He could only nod in reply, and with that he strode off.

Back in his tent he undressed quickly, and rolled underneath blankets that smelled of must and body odour. His mind whirled in thought. God be with you, Mrs. Schubert had said, with complete certainty that Providence might have a hand in protecting him. But sometimes he wondered. Though he had been raised a strict Presbyterian, and was usually pious to a fault, his faith eluded him periodically. During those moments he felt as if he were just going through the motions, as if something important had been disconnected, and it bothered him greatly. All he was really certain of at this juncture in his life was that Fortune was right when he had implied, back at Doherty's grave, that Death walked arm in arm with everyone, ready to stake a claim without notice. The best thing we can do in defiance, he reasoned, is live our lives with vigour. And isn't that really why we are here, in this very spot? And why we carry on?

He closed his eyes and saw the faces of Laura and the children, as clearly as if they had gathered beside him in the tent. She was such a good woman, her heart as big and open as the prairies, and she understood Thomas McMicking better than anybody and stuck by him regardless. That was what really made her a capital wife, that and the fact she was a good mother to their children, too. And oh, the children! How he missed them, missed being a father to them. They would need a father's love and a father's advice, and he wasn't there to give them either. It was the most lamentable part of this journey.

He fell asleep with the children on his mind, but he did not dream of them. He dreamed of the river, himself enveloped by it, without even the opportunity of filling his lungs with air before it sucked him down and down into the total blackness of oblivion. He awoke in a sweat, panting and filled with dread, the image frighteningly vivid in his mind. How many times had he dreamed about drowning on this trip? As many times as there had been a major river to cross. And none of those rivers were as formidable as the one he'd be facing come the dawn. Even worse, he wasn't just crossing it, he was rafting *down* it.

THE ROAD TO CARIBOO

Have you gazed on naked grandeur where there's
nothing else to gaze on ...
Black canyons where the rapids rip and roar?
Robert Service, "The Call of the Wild"

TÊTE JAUNE CACHE TO CARIBOO,
SEPTEMBER 1 — SEPTEMBER 7, 1862

P ower. That was what McMicking saw in this river. To
be sure, its beauty was unparalleled — an astonishing
green, unsullied as yet by the many tributaries that would
eventually join it on its quest for the sea — but there was more
to it than just beauty. Underneath that flat swirling surface was a
terrifying power, the power of a monster that could easily devour

them if it was not given due respect at all times. If we expect to reach Cariboo, he thought, we will do well to remember that, and never take this river for granted.

The weather had turned sombre. A cold front had pushed its way through the mountains overnight, a harbinger of winter, and dark, drizzling clouds hid the surrounding peaks. It was as if they were in a completely different country from the warm and sunny one they had inhabited only a few days before. The mountains now seemed like prison walls, and the green river the only pathway to freedom. The men's breath came out in grey puffs of condensation in the chilly, early-morning air, and McMicking's heart was pounding with apprehension as final preparations were made for departure. Some of us might not survive this run, he speculated, and tried not to think that if his life wasn't in God's hands then it was in his own, and he was determined not to be among the casualties. But he was shaken by the farewell words of one of the Indians: "Poor white men, no more," was what Cardinal translated.

One by one, over the course of the day, the rafts and canoes were pushed away from shore until they were caught in the current's muscular grasp. For safety's sake, generous gaps between departure times were allowed, and there were cries of "God speed" and "God bless" from those awaiting their turn. Besides a half-dozen canoes and an ox-hide boat, there were four single rafts, steered by large oars or sweeps, mounted in oarlocks on the stern, that were used as rudders, plus the two Huntingdon rafts that were lashed together bow to stern, with oarlocks and sweeps at each end, in case they broke apart. Lashed to the double raft's side was a 30-foot canoe. On board were 29 men, five tons of supplies, and four oxen, three horses

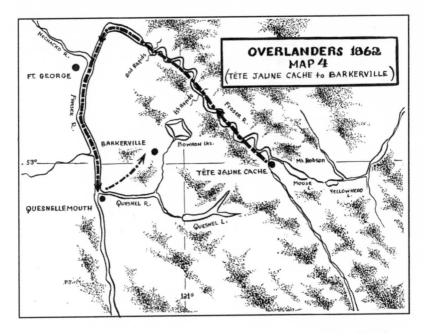

and two mules tied to a frame of rails built on the raft. The Queenston raft, and the others, were smaller versions of the same thing.

Soon the teepees were lost from view. The current was only running at five knots but, after walking more than a thousand miles, McMicking felt that the river banks were streaking by. The Fraser meandered at first, down the generous width of the Robson Valley, lined with scented pines and cottonwoods, but it wasn't long before it began to writhe like a snake between mountainsides that in places plunged straight into the water. Some of the bends were so sharp that every ounce of energy and diligence was required to keep the rafts from foundering on the rocky shores. This was especially true for the Huntingdon raft which

173

was as ponderous as an old bull elephant, and slow to respond to the sweep. Its deck was level with the surface of the river and the slightest bit of turbulence caused water to wash six inches deep over the top. Twice it got stuck on a rocky shoal; the animals had to be unloaded and the unwieldy vessel pried off. But beyond these problems the river was benign. Near day's end a canoe was sent off in advance to scout for a good camping spot, one that would provide reasonable foraging for the animals.

They floated on non-stop over the next couple of days, from dawn till dusk, Sellar's raft trailing McMicking's, between banks that were sometimes high and craggy and at other times densely forested right to the waterline. And always, the distance covered by land was only half of that covered on the river as it wound its way back and forth across the valley. In a bid to save time, fireplaces were built on board the rafts so that the men could cook without having to pull into shore. Then the valley opened up and the river widened, the curves became long and gentle and the current slowed down, so much that side sweeps had to be used as oars to help pick up speed. But generally there was so little to do that those not on watch, or rowing, managed to catnap the time away, under their rubber blankets in the wet weather that was accompanying them down the river. Some of the Huntingdon crew got sick from eating meat that had got contaminated, possibly from flies and the unsanitary conditions in which it was kept, and the resulting diarrhoea had them hanging over the stern of the raft.

Other than a couple of minor rapids that required close attention, there was clear sailing for two more days, and McMicking was beginning to relax a little. The notion of coming down this river had really unsettled him. He would have liked to take the North Thompson route with the Schuberts, but felt he owed his allegiance to the larger group running the Fraser. So far, he had no regrets: this was the easiest going that he and the others had had for months, and for the first time on their journey Cariboo actually seemed reachable. Then, on Thursday the mountains began to fence them in and the river to zigzag again. It was worrisome, but about all that had really changed was that the crew had to pay more attention to steering the raft than rowing it. The weather was still cold and wet, and the only sounds were the gurgle of the current, the hiss of water displaced by wood, the swish of the sweep and the odd complaint from an animal.

The first serious rapid to confront the Queenston raft was handled rather easily after the men scouted it out and planned the best way around a submerged rock at the entrance. The raft was more stable than McMicking had hoped as it surged through the canyon, seeming to take an extraordinarily long time to cover the short distance. He was elated when he came out at the bottom in smooth waters unscathed, with only trembling knees and wet feet to show for the experience.

They drifted along for a few more miles, the river very obliging, allowing them easy passage. Only sunny weather could have made the journey more enjoyable. If the rapids they had just negotiated were the worst the Fraser had to offer, then what was there to fear? Then a noise began to build in the distance, low at first, so that no one really noticed it. As it gradually increased and slowly penetrated minds that had been lulled into a false sense of security, the raft rounded a sharp turn and the noise became a startling roar that even a novice couldn't fail to recognize. It was the sound of great volumes of water being squeezed through a narrow opening.

Rapids. Major rapids, probably the great canyon the Indians had warned them about, the one that McMicking hoped they had already gone through. The lookout shouted, "Breakers ahead!"

The raft was picking up speed alarmingly. The crew scrambled madly to man the extra sweeps that were used when the river was slow; now they were needed for steering. The men jammed them in the water, pulling with all the strength they had, and slowly turned the lumbering craft into a relatively calm back eddy. One man leaped to shore and quickly snubbed the raft to a tree. They were safe for the moment, but had come within an inch of their lives of being swept into a maelstrom of water.

Once on shore, McMicking and the others were surprised to find three overlanders who had left Tête Jaune Cache earlier stranded there, without food or shelter. All were shivering from the cold and Eustache Pattison, the young man who had loaned Charles Racette his gun, was deathly ill. He'd had a sore throat back in Tête Jaune Cache, and exposure to the inclement weather had worsened it. Now he was burning up with fever. His companions explained how they had arrived here in their canoe two days before, having been the first to leave the Cache, and when they heard the rapids, managed to paddle safely to shore. They scouted downstream and decided it would be wise not to try to run the river. So they had tied a long rope to the canoe and attempted to track it down through the rapids, empty except for the provisions which they hoped would provide a degree of stability. In an instant the vessel was swamped and swept away, the rope torn from the men's hands by the raging torrent, and along with it went all of their food. They had been waiting here, half frozen and hungry, for someone to come along and save them, but they were beginning to think no one had made it past the first set of rapids, and that they were somehow going to have to walk to Fort George.

One of the Queenston men fetched some blankets and food for the trio, although Pattison was too ill to eat. "We've room for you on the raft, and plenty of food to see us through to Fort George," said McMicking, though he really wasn't sure of the truth of the latter part of his statement — no one knew how far it was to the HBC outpost.

McMicking and a few others climbed to the heights above the river for an overview of the rapids. All had seen rapids before, on the Niagara River, but never any like these. What they were looking upon was the Grand Canyon of the Fraser, a mile-long gouge in the land that consisted of a half-dozen razor-sharp turns and three distinct cataracts separated by comparatively smooth stretches. The precipitous canyon walls rose 250 feet above the water, and there was a claustrophobic feel to the place, in stunning contrast to the wide open spaces of the upper river. A churning torrent blasted its way through the defile like a battering ram, splintering into foam on massive boulders. Adding to the danger were submerged rocks that the water just skimmed over. They could capsize a small raft or canoe before the occupants had time to even think about avoiding them.

The men studied the canyon like fighters sizing up an opponent. The first rapid was the longest and the worst. The channel appeared to be no more than 60 feet across, with two sharp bends in it, and scarcely enough forward view to prepare for them. On the first bend a large rock protruded from the shore, causing the river to dip and rise on the open side as it surged around the obstruction. The drop in elevation from one end of the rapid to the other was astonishing; it looked more like a waterfall than a rapid to those with vivid imaginations. The river beat itself into shards against rock walls, and there were horrific whirlpools that looked capable of sucking just about anything into their depths. The rain and the ragged clouds that pressed down the slopes of the mountains made the canyon a dark, foreboding place, a place of doom. To McMicking, the water pouring through the chute looked like Death handing out invitations.

The men held council and decided that the wisest course was to run the raft through the first rapid with just enough men to handle it. The others would portage the supplies and animals to that point, after which they would have no choice but to return to the raft. There was no way to get the animals around the rest of the rapids. McMicking, his dreams of drowning all too clear in his mind, elected to help with the portage.

The raft was pushed off toward the cauldron of water. Then it was suddenly propelled forward and plunged wildly down the rapids, almost out of control, heaving and bucking like a wild animal. It passed so close to the big rock at the first bend that a sharp crack of wood could be heard above the thunder of water as the stern oar and lock were torn off. The men were horror-struck. The side sweeps tried to control the raft but it was in the firm grip of the river, which pushed it between two large whirlpools that grabbed at it, before shooting it into the calmer waters of the first pool. The crew whooped and shouted with jubilation while those on shore cheered loudly. It wasn't until he started to yell himself that McMicking realized his jaw was sore from clenching it so tightly.

The raft was snubbed and the oar-lock repaired while the animals and supplies were loaded on for the longer run down the last two rapids. McMicking had felt fear before, but not like this, and he couldn't help but think that this was where his nightmares were going to come true. There were prayers on everyone's lips as the raft was pushed off and picked up by the current. Providence was with them, however. The abundance of rain had resulted in a large run-off from the feeder streams and the river was deeper than usual. Still, the raft pitched and yawed, and was more than a foot under water at times. The men hung on for dear life, and McMicking swore that if he made it through this he would never question Providence again. His bowels felt mushy by the time the second pool was reached and without pausing, the raft was steered into the final cataract that rushed down through an even narrower part of the canyon. It looked like a cold version of Hell. The walls sped by, a wet blur of stone, and the helmsman was shouting orders at the side sweeps, but McMicking was conscious only of the roar of the water. At the bottom the raft was nearly sucked under by another giant whirlpool that held it for a moment, trying to decide whether or not to devour it, then catapulted the vessel into the smooth water that marked the end of the Grand Canyon of the Fraser.

McMicking could have collapsed with relief. When will this river ever end, he wondered, and would he see the end of it? Or would it see the end of him first?

Sellar and the Huntingdon party were several miles behind, drifting lazily toward the first cataract, when two heavily laden canoes, lashed together and showing only three inches of freeboard, passed them. The men called hellos to each other. It was Alexander Robertson, the surveyor from Goderich who had been one of the men elected captain back at Fort Pitt, with two other men, Robert

Warren and John Douglas. They had been the last to leave the Cache. Now they disappeared quickly around a bend in the river, leaving the Huntingdon raft to its solitary run.

Downstream, the canoeists discovered for themselves the many facets of this river. They heard the water funnelling through the canyon and experienced a moment of indecision. Should they drive to shore or continue? But it was too late. The canoes were so heavy and overloaded that the men could not maneuver out of the current. Before there was time for thought they were caught in the surging torrent and there was nothing they could do but face the consequences. Lacking the stability of the rafts, and having so little freeboard, they knew it wouldn't be an easy passage.

Robertson was steering from the stern, but couldn't control the awkward craft. It shot forward like a bullet from a gun, and just before entering the rapid it ran over a submerged boulder. It staggered momentarily, then rose, turned broadside to the current, rolled over and split apart. The men and provisions were spilled into the chaos of water and rocks. Robertson went flying off in one direction while the other men, neither of whom could swim, went off in another, along with the capsized vessels. Robertson, who was a strong swimmer, yelled at his companions, "Hang onto the canoe!" The men grabbed at it, but the vessel was tumbling over and over and was hard to hold on to. The waves beat them relentlessly, sucking them down and spitting them up, throwing them around like rag dolls. Robertson kept shouting words of encouragement that were choked off every time he was sucked beneath the turbulence. He clawed at the water as if it was something solid he could grab hold of, then he was shot up to the surface, gulping in air and bits of foam. Each time this happened he had less breath than before. His heavy wool pants and boots weighed him down, and the cold water numbed him. He became lethargic and the river smashed him against a rock, knocking the last of his breath from him. His world turned black; he slipped beneath the surface and did not rise again.

Somehow the other two men got safely through the canyon, to the relatively calm stretch of water, and were caught up on a gravel bar about a half mile downstream. They dragged themselves from the water, half frozen, utterly exhausted and battered from the rocks. Douglas was barely alive, and Warren in only slightly better shape. However, he was mobile and, shivering uncontrollably, he hurried along the edge of the bar to see if he could spot Robertson dragging himself up on shore somewhere. He saw no one and heard no cries for help. There was only the flotsam from the canoe gliding by in the grey light of the canyon, as if someone had dumped their garbage somewhere upstream. His friend was gone, carried away forever by the unforgiving river.

Meanwhile, the Huntingdon raft easily shot the rapids and when the crew saw the two men stranded on the island, Alexander Fortune and another man untied the long canoe and pushed out into the river to rescue them. The current was fierce, but a few swift strokes with the paddles had the canoe scraping onto the gravel bar. It was as welcome a sound as Warren and Douglas had ever heard.

Sellar and the remainder of the crew tried to snub the raft near the island, but the current was too strong. As they were pulled inexorably downstream, Fortune yelled at them to keep an eye out for Robertson. The raft had gone a mile before a quiet back eddy was found in which to tie up. They saw no sign of the missing man anywhere along the way. Sellar hurried back along the bank hoping to spot him, hoping that perhaps he would find the man clinging to a rock at the water's edge, exhausted but alive. He saw nothing but the heedless river gurgling through the desolate country. Never in his life had he felt so helpless.

Eventually, Fortune and the others were reunited with the raft. Both Warren and Douglas were in shock from the icy waters and the loss of their good friend. They reckoned he must have cramped up from the cold, his body caught somewhere on an invisible snag. A search was made for the lost provisions in hopes of salvaging something, but the river had swept them away too. A profound sense of disbelief and doom hung over everyone in this remote corner of the earth, beneath the funereal sky, in the chilly rain. And the question, unspoken among them, was, "Who will be the next to be claimed by this river?"

When at last they shoved off from shore they were changed men. Gone was the complacency that most had slipped into, the growing feeling that the Fraser would bring them unharmed to their destination. Now there was real fear, fear of what awaited them beyond each new bend in the river. Everyone was on guard then, when they heard the rush of the water through the Grand Canyon of the Fraser. They tied up and when they viewed the rocky slit in the earth from above, it stunned them. It was so fearsome, so overwhelming that Sellar estimated its walls to be 500 feet high, more than twice their actual height.

Still, the raft had to be taken through, and there was no avoiding it. As the Queenston men had done earlier, the Huntingdon crew decided that it would be wiser if only a few of them were on board during the first stage of the rapids while the rest portaged around it. Ten men, including Sellar, volunteered for raft duty, and there wasn't one of them who didn't think that the water roaring through the narrow canyon might very well be the death of them all. They launched the raft with an uneasy fatalism.

It was a roller-coaster ride that saw the vessel nearly caught up among the rocks and smashed to bits. Rounding the elbow of the first big rock, one side of the raft rolled up so high that Sellar feared it might turn right over. But in an instant they were carried by, the sheer size of the raft bulling them through. Then its length became a curse. It got caught up across the two whirlpools, which the Queenston raft had passed between. The men worked the sweeps furiously, up to their knees in water, and for the longest time the vessel seemed to be held there, the force of the water trying to tear it apart. Then it lunged forward into quieter waters.

They snubbed the raft and picked up the others who had been watching the adventure with awe, certain they would have to begin rescue operations and thankful it was unnecessary. Like the Queenston men, they cheered wildly once the raft was through.

They ran the second rapid successfully, giving themselves over to Providence and the helmsman. They went through pell-mell, a heartbeat away from being dashed on the rocks, the raft so far under water at times that a spectator might have thought there wasn't one. In the grip of the last rapid they were momentarily hung up on some rocks and nearly torn apart. But the torrent that had pushed them on pushed them off again, and they squeezed through to the bottom of the canyon where the whirlpools tried to swamp them for good. Their size was helpful, too much even for this river to handle, and the raft lumbered out like a broaching whale. They coasted into a silence that was almost deafening.

McMicking breathed a sigh of relief as the river broadened again. Soon it grew sluggish and the distance between its banks lent it the appearance of a lake. They ran at night to make up for the time they had lost at the rapids and due to the slow pace of the river. The men took turns on watch, looking out for shoals or any other danger the river might have in store for them. In the early hours of the morning they ran into fog so thick the helmsman couldn't see to steer and they were forced to pull into shore until visibility improved enough to show the way. The river remained wide and calm but the fog never completely lifted. They passed between heavily timbered shores, and in the grey, misty light McMicking saw it as a lonely, forlorn place. What's more, their food supplies were nearly gone and they were down to eating meat with only a miserly ration of flour. He worried that they would get sick from eating flyblown meat but it was all they had to keep them going. The lack of proper nutrition affected their energy level but at least they weren't having to expend much on this part of their journey. The river was doing most of the work for them.

The weather remained cold and wet, and keeping warm with no work to do was a problem. Everyone was eager to take a turn manning the sweeps. One night, when they had had enough of being miserable, they tied up to the shore and built a huge fire to ease the chill in their bones. The animals were left to forage in the parsimonious forest. Around the fire the men spoke openly of their feelings about the future, its uncertainty and the profound homesickness they felt. Some were so stricken by the malady they said they were going to head directly home without stopping to look for gold. A few said they wished they had never left. Robert Warren, fully recovered from his near drowning in the river, was disgusted by such talk.

"How can you even think about returning," he said to them, "after all the hardship you've endured? As far as I'm concerned, finding some Cariboo gold is the only way to make up for it!"

The argument went on into the night, but Warren was unable to change the minds of those who had come to learn that real wealth had little to do with an element from the ground.

Back on the river by six in the morning, the discussion turned to how far it was to Fort George. McMicking insisted that it couldn't be very far along the river, 50 to 100 miles, perhaps less if the map they had was correct.

"So it's possible," one of the more optimistic men said, "that we might reach the fort this afternoon."

"It's possible," replied McMicking, "provided we don't encounter any more rapids."

But the map was at best only an approximation of their route, at worst a pack of lies. The afternoon came and went and there was no sign of Fort George. There were, however, more rapids.

The river had been fairly sluggish, but the next day they reached a long stretch of rough water that went on for 15 miles. There were rocks strewn everywhere. It was like steering through a maze, and eventually the raft got hung up on a large boulder and would not budge. The men quickly secured ropes to the bow and stern, then two good swimmers took the other ends to shore and tied them to a tree. Once that was done, McMicking and the others began cutting the raft in half by slashing through the ropes holding the logs together. Then they waited. Slowly at first, the river pulled them from the rock, then in a rush the two smaller parts were swept in an arc to the shore. The men on board were nearly knocked into the water as the halves collided. Leaping to the bank they hauled the two pieces together and re-lashed them. This undertaking held them up for five hours.

McMicking cursed the delay. Eustache Pattison's condition was worsening. He was burning up with fever, working hard for every breath, and there was nothing Dr. Stevenson could do for him. He suspected diphtheria. They had to get the young man to the fort and hope there was something there that could help him.

The mood of the river changed once again, and the raft drifted idly along, hemmed in by huge stands of cottonwoods. But the land itself was opening up into low rolling hills with the real mountains providing a distant backdrop towards the southeast and the west. By mid-morning of the next day the buildings of Fort George at last hove into view. It was Monday, September 8, eight long days out of Tête Jaune Cache.

The first thing McMicking attended to was getting Pattison into the fort. The youngster was barely alive, his breathing even more laboured. They made him as comfortable as possible in a small storage shed, but he was beyond all help and died that night at nine o'clock, as if someone had choked the life out of him.

The following morning Sellar, Fortune and the Huntingdon raft arrived, the last of the original party that had left Fort Garry on June 2. McMicking greeted them with the sad news of Pattison's death. When Sellar told him of Robertson's drowning, McMicking was heart-stricken. So many months, over such a long distance, and not a man lost, and now, in less than a week two of their finest young men were gone. And with the goldfields only a stone's throw away. The irony was almost unbearable.

There were no boards available at the fort so the men cut one of the smaller canoes in half to use as a coffin. They buried Pattison just outside the garrison walls, in a small parcel of land that had recently been set aside as a cemetery. A cold mist hung in the air as Fortune said the eulogy, and finished up with the 23rd Psalm. Then with great sorrow, they lowered the coffin slowly into the ground.

There were tears on McMicking's cheeks. If this was God's judgment, then where was the sense in it?

There was little point in lingering at this pathetic outpost of civilization, particularly with their ultimate goal so close. Besides, there was a shortage of provisions at the fort and the factor was unable to supply the overlanders with the food they needed to complete their journey. A couple of the men stole some potatoes and turnips from the fields outside the fort, while others bartered with the local Indians for bear, beaver and badger meat. They also acquired as much smoked salmon and dried berries as they could afford.

On the morning of September 10 both rafts left the fort. The river between here and Quesnellemouth was well charted, and they knew they were only two days' sail from their destination.[1] They also knew that they had two more rapids to run on the way down. The factor had said that the rafts might not make it through, but the consensus was that they had to try their luck anyway. They hired two Indians with canoes to go with them to the first canyon, to help with a rescue should the rafts be wrecked.

They ran swiftly, due south now, and unhindered. The weather had cleared and the day was sunny and warm for a change, not the kind of day to give much credence to dying.

The first series of rapids ran a crooked path among a chain of small rocky islands, most of them capped with evergreen trees. The rafts were snubbed and the channel investigated. They could clearly see that if they stuck to the left side of the river there was a good chance of making it through, even with the small waterfall and whirlpool at the bottom. For safety's sake it was decided that most of the men would walk around the rapids. The animals, however, would have to stay on the rafts since the terrain was far too rugged for them. Unwilling to press his luck, McMicking chose the overland route.

With just enough men to handle them, the rafts shot through one at time. They careered over the fall, where each was caught up by the whirlpool and spat out. Because of its size the Huntingdon raft sank alarmingly in the eddy so that the men were waist deep in swirling water, and the animals were up to their chests. For a moment Sellar was sure they were doomed. Time stopped: the raft was suspended beneath the surface of the brown water. All that kept the animals on board were their tethers. The men hung on for dear life. Then the whirlpool ejected them, as if the mass of logs was nothing more than a bunch of matchsticks.

The powerful current carried the rafts four miles downstream before the crews could snub them to pick up their companions.

Farther downstream they saw prospectors working the river bank for gold, and pulled in. The men were Chinese, the first that many of the overlanders had ever seen. They had discouraging news. Not only was the mining season about to come to a close, the cost of living in Cariboo was prohibitive. Miners were flocking south to the coast like migrating birds, most of them broke and many half-starved.

The next morning the weather was unco-operative. Fog came and went, forcing the rafts into shore. It was late in the afternoon before they reached the second rapid, but they sailed through it without a problem.[2] A mile and a half of rough water, and the worst that the Fraser had to offer was behind them. In less than three quarters of an hour they were tying up at Quesnellemouth, 100 days out of Fort Garry.

Stepping on shore, most of the men paused for a moment and, bowing their heads, gave thanks to God for their safe arrival. McMicking was exhilarated that he had actually made it. His dreams had been so vivid. Yet here he was, beyond the river's dangerous grasp, alive, all of his dreams apparently nothing more than figments of an over-active imagination.

It was a lovely spot, this small settlement at the confluence of the Fraser and Quesnel rivers, especially now with the cottonwoods and aspens brilliant with fall colours. Even better, just 50 miles or so to the east, an easy walk for these men, was Williams Creek and the rapidly expanding mining town of Barkerville, although that was not a name with which the men were familiar. However, it was the place for which they had left their homes and families and all things dear to them, more than four and a half months ago, the place that had lured them across 1,300 miles of prairies and rugged mountains, fording and rafting rivers, at times soaked in sweat in the withering heat of the summer sun, at other times soaked in rain, or waist deep in sloughs and bogs, not to mention harried by the voracious insects that feasted on them most of the way. Such a long road, that had served up so many privations and offered more risks to life and limb than most men would face in a lifetime. And two good men lost forever, holes in the lives of their loved ones that would never be adequately filled. But for the lucky ones, it was all behind them now. They were here. They had done it.

McMicking's mind drifted to Catherine Schubert. Where was she now? If the weather had been as foul for her party as it had for his, she'd be having a time of it and that was for sure.

But if there was a woman more capable of putting one foot in front of the other when the world was shouting "Stop!" then he'd like to meet her. Still, the smallest piece of news would have been most welcome.

THE ROAD TO FORT KAMLOOPS

'Tis the song, the sigh of the weary
Hard Times, Hard Times, come again no more
Many days you have lingered around my cabin door
Oh, Hard Times, come again no more.

Stephen Foster, "Hard Times"

TÊTE JAUNE CACHE TO FORT KAMLOOPS,
SEPTEMBER 2 — OCTOBER 14, 1862

The Schuberts watched with stirred-up emotions as McMicking and the others set off down the Fraser. Wrapped in a shawl, Catherine held James in her arms and realized that she was squeezing him tighter than usual. She was tense, and breathed deeply to try to relax. She had formed bonds with many of the men, especially McMicking, and would miss them terribly. It was as if a part of her family was sailing away, and only God knew if their paths would ever cross again. She hoped so. Yet if the world came between them as this river had, she would still count Thomas McMicking as one of her friends. Her sense of loss was heightened by the dreary weather that pressed down on the valley. She and Augustus stood there silently as the rafts disappeared from sight, quickly and smoothly, and momentarily wondered why they had chosen the longer overland route. Then they began preparing for their own departure.

Later that evening her thoughts turned to Sellar. What a strange man he was. When he had brought her the pemmican she thought he'd had a change of heart, but soon realized what he was up to. So she wasn't surprised that when he left he hadn't bothered to say goodbye. It was probably just his way of letting her know once more where she stood. Ah, well. An energetic man on his feet, a lazy man in his head, and that was the long and short of him.

If it was any consolation, one of the Shuswaps had agreed to guide them as far as the headwaters of the North Thompson, and that meant that they would also have the services of André Cardinal for a while. His quiet confidence and enviable competence had been a boon to everyone during the long trek to this valley. There are some men, Catherine thought, who have a knack for always choosing the right thing to do. McMicking was one and Cardinal was another. She was glad he was accompanying them.

On Tuesday, September 2, the North Thompson party set out to meet its own fate. Having crossed the Fraser River the day before, nearly three dozen of them, with three times that many animals, struck out along a trail that followed the McLennan

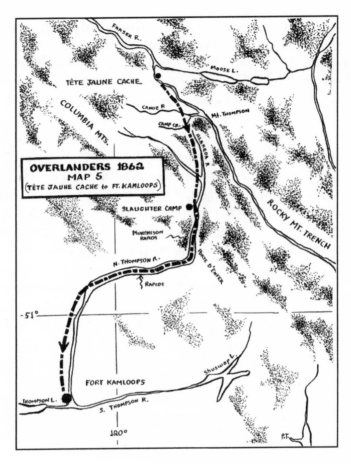

River, a tributary of the Fraser. Made by the Indians, the trail was in reasonably good shape. Still, it was not suitable for riding, so the party moved along on foot, herding the cattle and leading their horses. Catherine carried four-year-old Mary Jane on her back; Augustus carried Gus Jr., who would soon be six, while others in the group took turns carrying James, two and a half.

The country they passed through was open and pleasant, joined by small, grassy side-valleys. Beyond a shallow lake dotted with reedy islets loomed the barren, glaciated peak and gentle slopes of Mount Thompson, the vanguard of the Malton Range.[1] It was flanked to the left by the great Rocky Mountain Trench and the Canoe River, and to the right by a smaller valley cut by Camp Creek. The Shuswap guide, who had thus far proven himself quite useless, was at least helpful with his advice to ignore the broad trench, which was a continuation of the trail they were on, and to branch off to the right, along Camp Creek, instead. First, however, they had to cross the Canoe River.

A tributary of the Columbia, the Canoe River was just 15 miles from the Cache, but it took the party two full days to reach it. The river had worn a deep groove in the earth, and its banks were high and steep. A trail had to be hacked diagonally down to the water, through a thick forest where huge swarms of mosquitoes had gathered as if they had been waiting a lifetime for such a banquet to come their way.

Catherine faced these mountain rivers with great trepidation and concern for the safety of the children. Unlike the prairie rivers, which were benign by comparison, these were dangerous, much more likely to carry a person off if they weren't careful. Not only were they swifter, they were about as cold as water could be without being solid ice. Still, if there was ever a group of people well practised in the art of river crossing, it surely had to be this one preparing to cross the Canoe. Catherine tried to tally up the rivers they had crossed between here and Fort Garry, but lost count. Whatever the number, it was at least one too many.

The men built rafts while Cardinal drove the animals into the glacial water and swam them across. The river was high because of recent rains, and running at a good pace, but the crossing was made without incident. On the far side, another diagonal trail had to be cut up the equally steep south bank, through an equally thick forest with just as many blood-sucking mosquitoes wanting to feast on them.

They located Camp Creek, a tributary of the Canoe, and followed it, over open rocky ground for a while, then up into a narrow, densely wooded valley, painstakingly clearing a path for themselves and the animals, and battling with insects. The trail, difficult to begin with, had now deteriorated into a nightmare of rocks, fallen timber and thick underbrush. The effort required to get the animals past these obstacles sapped everyone's strength, and the pace was accordingly slow. Catherine wondered how her exertions were affecting the baby. She could feel it stirring inside her, sometimes as if in protest, and there were moments when it seemed that she might give birth right here. Having delivered three children already, she knew it wasn't its time, but these were unusual circumstances that could easily provoke an entirely unexpected outcome. And wouldn't that surprise some of these men! In a way, she felt dishonest, but she didn't think her condition was something to which they needed to be privy.

Leaving Camp Creek behind, the party continued south, up to a broad ridge that was actually a small divide. On top was a marshy lake that looked like it had once drained from both ends. The north end was plugged by a beaver dam, but the south end flowed out to become the Albreda River. Here, the Shuswap indicated that he would go no farther. No objections were raised. His advice had been scant, and his participation in the onerous task of creating a trail negligible. It was this failing that offended the overlanders the most.

On the far side of the ridge the party descended along the Albreda which, the Shuswap had told Cardinal, would eventually join the North Thompson, a dozen or so miles farther down the valley — another two or three days' travel at the pace they were moving. Much of the route was through a dense forest of enormous cedars and pines. They passed two gigantic cedar trees growing from a common base, the circumference of which was nearly 40 feet. Many others were six to eight feet in diameter. Here and there were thickets of prickly devil's club, taller than a man, and there was bear spoor everywhere, though they had yet to spot any of the creatures. Grouse were so plentiful and unaffected by humans they could be knocked down with a stick. Every now and then a muskeg had to be waded, which slowed the party down even more, and a tributary of the Albreda that had to be forded was slippery and dangerous. By the time they reached the North Thompson, they had been on the trail from the Cache for a week and had covered less than 40 miles.

Cardinal said that it was now time for him to take his leave. He assured the men and Catherine that all they had to do was stick close to the river, following it downstream, and it would take them to Fort Kamloops, another 170 miles or so to the south. It was a sad parting of the ways, for the company hated to see him go. The guide had won the admiration of everyone, and he was given three rousing cheers as he disappeared up the trail. Augustus carved the details of his departure into a tree trunk: "Andre Cardinal departed Sep 12 1862." For the second time on their long journey, the overlanders were on their own.

Near the junction of the two rivers the men built rafts, and from a calm, sandy cove launched them across the green waters of the North Thompson. Setting out on the far side, they discovered they had actually landed on an island. This elicited moans, but at least the southern fork was narrow and could be forded. However, it would have to wait. Night was falling.

At dawn they crossed to the other bank and clawed their way up a steep bluff to the high ground above the river, where they paused for a bit. Before Cardinal had turned toward home, he had presented the overlanders with a tantalizing alternative. If they were to turn *up* the North Thompson, which at this point poured out of the mountains from the northwest, it was only 150 miles to the gold creeks of Cariboo. Other than the approximate distance, he had no knowledge of the terrain, although he had heard it would not be an easy passage. Nonetheless, it was an exciting idea. Should they try that route instead? If it was passable, they might conceivably reach their destination in two weeks. On the other hand, continuing south at their present rate would probably mean having to wait till spring to get to Cariboo. There was some discussion about what to do, and the possibility that they could be digging for gold in a fortnight had strong appeal. A consensus was reached; they would go upstream and see what came of it.

A large portion of the day was spent forcing their way along the south shore, axing through the thick bush and deadfall, their pace slower than a crawl. Then they came to a ravine that might as well have been a brick wall, so impossible was it for the animals to negotiate. Looking across the river the men could see that the terrain there wasn't any better. Others scouted up the ravine for another route, but found nothing. They hated to give up, but the way wasn't fit for man nor beast. Deflated, they set up camp and the next morning retraced their steps to where the North Thompson bent south on its run to Fort Kamloops.

The southern route was almost as difficult. They worked from dawn till dusk, day in and day out, with little progress to show for it, and because they moved slowly, they were forced to work all the harder. Finally, they had all had enough. They were 17 days out of the Cache and they estimated that they had come just 60 miles. That amounted to a paltry three and a half miles a day![2] At this rate they would never reach Fort Kamloops before winter came, and they knew with deadly certainty that when the snow flew in this valley it would block their way like a jail door slamming shut. It was frightening to contemplate, the kind of thing that tied the gut in a knot. There wasn't one of these weary souls who hadn't heard of the Donner party and its horrific ordeal in the Sierra Nevada Mountains during the winter of 1846-47. If they wanted to avoid a similar fate they had better take drastic action and take it fast.

After camp was set up, a meeting was held. Complaints were heard and they were numerous. No one had expected the trail to be as rough as it was, nor that they would be on it so long. If they were going to make Fort Kamloops before winter set in, it was obvious that they needed to start putting more miles behind them. In the end, there was only one solution to their problem. They must slaughter the cattle for food, abandon most of the horses, build rafts and canoes and take to the river, with prayers that it would offer a kinder passage.

Some were frightened at the mere thought of such a venture. They had come this way because they couldn't swim and were afraid of the water. Furthermore, *nothing* was known of this river, unlike the Fraser, about which the Indians were able to impart at least some intelligence. They would be like blind men feeling their way down a path never before trod. Yet everyone realized it was the only realistic course of action open to them. They faced either a dangerous river that might kill them, or a winter that surely would.

With their minds made up, the men set to work early the following morning. Some began butchering animals while others fell trees for rafts and dugouts. The small area of wilderness they occupied was filled with a cacophony of axes thudding against wood, bawling oxen and human voices raised to be heard above the din. Catherine tended one of the fires and jerked meat. She was in a quandary about taking to the river. In one way she was relieved to see an end to the punishment her body had been subjected to over the last few days, while in another, she was sure that the river placed the children in greater danger. Granted, the two oldest were tired of being carried almost everywhere, and were even excited about the prospects of a raft journey, but it filled Catherine with worry. She would not despair, though. She would meet tomorrow and the next day, and every day after that, with the same resolve she faced today and yesterday, and it would see her and the children through. And surely God would not desert them.

In the midst of all the activity, another party of overlanders arrived from the north. Some were stragglers from the McMicking party who had fallen behind on the way to the Cache, including Bill Morrow, now fully recovered, albeit scarred, from his second encounter with an ox back in Lac Ste. Anne. The others were a party of Americans from St. Peters, Minnesota, who had left Fort Garry five days after McMicking. Like their compatriots, who journeyed west to Oregon and California in covered wagons pulled by mules, the St. Peters men crossed the Canadian prairies in the same fashion, the only group known to do so. The two parties had brought with them 30 animals, horses and oxen —

the mules had been traded away in Fort Edmonton — which boosted the count that had to be dealt with to 130.

For three days everyone laboured untiringly, killing oxen, jerking meat and building rafts and canoes. On the one hand they were grateful for the respite from the trail, but on the other, they fretted because they were not moving. Speculation about what might await them between here and Fort Kamloops was rampant.

On the eve of their departure a hush fell over the camp as everyone turned in early with their own ruminations on the subject. If Mr. McMicking were here, mused Catherine, he'd probably have us singing, perhaps Stephen Foster's "Hard Times," but singing nonetheless. She wondered where he and the others were at this very moment, if Providence had guided them safely to Cariboo. She prayed it was so, and she prayed that a benevolent God would sail with her and all the others in the morning. She turned on her side and Augustus pulled her close to him, and there was much comfort in his touch.

The night was clear and cold, a welcome change from the grey, sometimes sodden skies they had been under most of the way here. In the moonlight that flooded the clearing, the ground glimmered with frost. The river tumbled by, the white riffles on its surface turned silver in the light. The sound of the water hid the sounds of the forest, and for some that was a good thing. For others it was simply a ceaseless reminder of the dangers they would be facing come the dawn.

The camp was awake early on Monday, September 22. Excitement, as tangible as the river, permeated the camp as rafts and canoes were loaded with baggage and the animals that had been spared. Pack saddles, harnesses and other unnecessary paraphernalia that were left strewn about the empty campsite would mark the overlanders' passage through this spot for years to come.[3] Bill Morrow wrote in heavy pencil on a tree: "Slaughter Camp, Sep 22 1862," then the party shoved off into the current of the North Thompson, mercifully unaware that during McMicking's perilous journey down the Fraser the river had greedily swallowed up one of their own.

The first two days on the North Thompson were slow and arduous, the pace not much faster than it had been on land. The water was shallow, with numerous gravel bars that necessitated unloading the rafts in order to get them across. Just as bad were snags of driftwood that had to be cleared before further headway was possible. On the third day the river opened up a little and became more accommodating. The rafts and canoes drifted smoothly south, strung out over a considerable distance at irregular intervals.

Swiftly rounding a bend in the river, one of the larger rafts, carrying a dozen men and seven horses, got caught up on a snag. A smaller raft, with four men — William Hugill, William Fortune (no relation to Alexander), Archibald Thompson and John Fannin — their horses, and a dog, was unable to steer clear and bumped into the larger one, dislodging it before getting stuck itself. Other rafts approached, but sailed by when the stranded men waved them on, shouting that they didn't need assistance. They would free the vessel themselves and catch up.

But that was more easily said than done. Try as they might, they couldn't move the raft, and there was no place to get a good purchase to lift it off. All they could do was abandon the vessel and try to catch up with their companions on foot, praying that they wouldn't encounter any insurmountable obstacles on the way.

The horses were driven into the water so they could swim to shore, then the men crawled across the tangle of trees in the snag, and the dog followed. Leaving the horses to fend for themselves in the wilderness, the quartet began working their way along the shoreline, hoping that the others were waiting for them only a short distance downstream. But the terrain was an obstacle course of rocks and fallen trees, and stubbornly resisted their passage every step of the way. By the time darkness set in they had put only two miles behind them, and there was nothing to do but camp for the night.

Camping was not a choice they would have made under different circumstances. They had neither food nor blankets — those items had preceded them down river on a different raft — but they at least had the dog, and knives to carve it up for food if it became necessary. They also had matches and got a good fire blazing, huddling around it for warmth. It rained throughout much of the night.

By morning, everyone was grumpy, having hardly slept a wink. Their bellies were rumbling and they were hungry enough to kill the dog for breakfast, but held off, hoping someone would come to their assistance. They stayed put till noon, the hours as heavy as lead, but no one came. They could have been the last four men on earth for all they knew. Then one of the men noticed a remarkable thing. Wasn't the river much higher than it had been the day before? There were rocks along the shore that hadn't been covered when the men arrived last night, and now they were. The river had risen a good six inches, and that held an exciting possibility: that they might have a chance of getting the raft off the snag. They hurried back upstream as quickly as the land would allow, the dog leading the way.

The raft was teetering on the snag in the high water and came off with little difficulty. Indeed, another inch or two of water and there might not have been a raft there to come back to. They snubbed up to the bank a few yards downstream and gathered the horses, which had not wandered far over the rugged terrain.

It was late afternoon before they pushed off into the current in a bid to catch up with their companions. They were ravenous, and with every passing mile the dog began to look more and more appetizing. Finally, in the dregs of the day, they came upon the rest of their party, anxiously awaiting their arrival but fearing the worst had happened. They had had no means of sending a search party back to find Hugill and his companions.

The next day, September 27, the rafts were away at first light and made excellent progress during the morning. However, by one o'clock in the afternoon there were formidable rapids ahead.

Like many geographical features on the trip thus far, they were unnamed, but they would become known as the Murchison Rapids. Those who had seen them would never again hear the name without a flutter of the heart. They ran through a narrow canyon nine miles in length. Near the bottom end of the canyon the sides closed in even further, to a span of 15 yards, and made a sharp right turn between near-vertical rock walls. All of the water carried down a river that was normally 30 to 60 yards wide was funnelled through this slit at a horrifying velocity; it would be named appropriately *Porte d'Enfer,* or "Little Hell's Gate." But unlike its larger cousin on the Fraser River, which could be run by river craft, this stretch of water was simply not navigable.

One by one the vessels pulled into shore. The big raft, carrying the 12 men and 7 horses was unwieldy in the strong current, and the men who jumped ashore were not able to snub it. Several other men leapt into the river and scrambled to shore, but two men did not get off in time. They and the animals rushed toward the turbulent water.

The man trying desperately to steer the raft was John Fannin. There was a big rock sticking up right at the entrance to the rapids and he headed for it, not knowing exactly what he would do when he got there, just that it was the only piece of solid ground in the vicinity. The raft was hard to control in the swift water and smashed headlong into the rock. Before Fannin's eyes the bindings around the logs began to snap and the raft to fall apart. He and his companion were able to scramble to safety on the boulder while the torn-apart raft and the horses were carried off in the chaos of water.

On shore, Andrew Holes, a 26-year-old New Yorker, grabbed a line, tied one end to a tree and the other to himself and climbed into a dugout. He paddled out to midstream, then drifted toward the rock while some men on shore took up the slack in the rope to prevent him from sharing the raft's fate. With some tricky maneuvering he reached the boulder and was able to get both men safely into the canoe. Then the others on shore reeled them in like a big fish, hand over hand.

Just then another raft came down river, this one carrying four men. Those on shore shouted warnings of the rapids ahead, Catherine's voice rising above them. The men struggled to get their raft in to the bank, but it was a vessel designed for floating, not for maneuverability, and they only managed to get within a few yards. Two men made a split-second decision and jumped into the river to try swimming to shore. Both were strong, but the water was cold and the current powerful, and only one was able to make it. The river took the other, still fighting for his life, into the mouth of the canyon and the tumultuous water. In an instant he was gone.

Catherine screamed in horror. When the raft with the other two men on it also disappeared into the chute, her legs turned wobbly and she grabbed Augustus' arm for support. "Oh, Jesus, Mary and Joseph!" she gasped, and her shoulders sagged as she crossed herself and begged God to save their souls. Augustus took her in his arms and held her tightly, as much for his comfort as for hers.

Meanwhile, the raft carrying the two men, both petrified with fear, went hurtling down the rapids, bouncing off rocks that almost spilled them a dozen times. For two long miles they were at the river's mercy, but hung on until the vessel was finally caught up on a snag. Then they clambered ashore as easily as if they had tied up to a fine wharf, wholly astonished by their good fortune. They looked for their companion, but knew in their hearts that he belonged to the river. Sadly, it was William Strachan, the man whose valiant efforts on the South Saskatchewan had brought James Kelso back from death's door.

The overlanders, of course, did not know what awaited them at the end of the canyon; in fact, they had no idea of the canyon's length. But it didn't matter. There was no way under God's grey skies that anyone wanted to challenge those harrowing waters. They prepared for a portage. All the goods were removed from the rafts which were then pushed out into the current, with hopes that some might survive the journey to the end of the rapids, wherever that might be. (Two of them were caught on snags on the way down, and the rest were smashed into driftwood.)

The party moved off in a pall of gloom, worsened by the dismal weather. A cold rain pelted down, eventually turning to sleet, and then to snow. The route above the canyon was as rough a trail as they had ever encountered. It was strewn with fallen timber and slick rocks and not an inch of it was level ground. There were steep side-hills slippery with sharp scree that tortured their feet, but they were the only way around cliffs that plunged vertically to the river far below. Visibility was limited by the weather and they could not tell how far they'd come or how far they had to go to reach the end of the canyon — if there was an end.

On the first day their spirits were lifted by finding Strachan's companions waiting patiently for them to show up. The two men were unharmed, and had been able to climb out of the canyon without too much difficulty. All the horses that plummeted down the rapids also survived, but could not be rescued. They were left to whatever fate might befall them.

The gurgle of the river below and the thwack of axes filled the wilderness as the party inched its way forward. Clearing a path was gruelling work so the men took turns, but the worst part of it was when they stopped and lost the body heat they had built up. It made them feel twice as cold and amplified their aches and pains. Occasionally they had to remove the animals' loads to reduce the risk of a broken leg. For three days the party traversed the mountainsides in rain and snow, chopping through fallen trees, slipping and sliding down into gullies and climbing back up the other side, collecting cuts and bruises as easily as wool collects burrs. Progress was marked off in increments of misery, but all they could do was keep moving forward one exhausting step at a time. They dared not look back; it was dispiriting as they could see few indications of movement. Nights were spent huddled around small fires beneath makeshift lean-tos because there were no spaces large enough or level enough on which to pitch a tent. Morale in the company sagged badly. Their only solace was in the recollection of past contentments, and the hope that they might come out of this alive.

When she slept, if such a word was appropriate, Catherine dreamed of flying, her arms spread, soaring through bright sunlight above wide open spaces. If only she could have done it! She would have gathered her family and flown as far from this place as it was possible to go and she would never return, not for all the gold in the world. But the dreary reality of her life was an irregular line of tree and rock-covered mountainsides, melding in the near distance with low clouds fat and dark with rain and snow. And it never seemed to change.

How many times, she wondered, had she asked herself what she was doing here? Why she was risking her life — more important, her children's lives — just to be with this man who was her husband and who dreamed of gold? Whatever had possessed her back in Fort Garry to insist that she be part of this journey? Surely a passage around Cape Horn in the most violent of storms would be better. Anything would be better than this. Now the child inside her was growing more active with each passing day. How she would love to expel it, to rid her body of it, but not here, not in this unforgiving place where it seemed even God had turned his back on her.

Sometimes she escaped from the daily torture by moving on to another plane of existence, a place where her mind was disconnected from her body. She knew it was she herself going through all the motions, yet somehow it wasn't. Wherever this place might be, it was beyond pain, beyond exhaustion, a world where such things were temporarily suspended. Then something would jar her back to reality, back to just wanting to give up, to tell Augustus that she would go no farther, that it was easier to die than it was to take another step. But she persisted, not knowing what kept her going, whether it was Augustus urging her on or her children or simply a primitive biological need to survive.

Augustus himself felt about ready to collapse from fatigue though he was not a man who tired easily. Besides Catherine and the children, all that was driving him forward was anger. He was angry at himself for not putting up a better argument when Catherine insisted on coming on this journey. Even knowing that arguing with her was like trying to blow out a prairie fire did nothing to improve his mood. Had he not relented, she and the children would be safe now and he would have fewer things to worry about. He cursed himself for being as soft as bread dough, and he cursed the other source of his anger: a throbbing tooth that even the oil of cloves no longer helped. He was ready to ask someone with pliers and a strong hand to pull it out for him. He whacked angrily at a thick branch with his machete, slicing it clean through with one blow, and felt slightly better for it.

Then, as if in sympathy, a hole in the clouds opened above them and the sun shone through. The warmth was a reprieve, and they stopped to let it wash over them — and it felt like sinking into a warm bath. Soon the valley broadened and the ground levelled out, with nothing to climb over, clear away or go around, which, to Catherine, was almost as good as a street in an eastern city. When the company saw the horror of Porte d'Enfer, it offered some consolation for the killing effort to reach and pass beyond it.

Three days. Nine miles. Three days of *rations* to go nine miles. Now their food supplies were severely depleted and they were faced with the possibility of death by starvation. If they ever hoped to see Fort Kamloops they had to build more rafts, so they wasted no time in falling trees, stripping them and lashing them together. They worked into the night by firelight, and were on the river the next day.

For several miles the North Thompson was relatively wide but shallow. Then it narrowed again into a long series of moderate rapids near the end of which was a small waterfall that none of the rafts could negotiate. The overlanders off-loaded all the goods by rope, and abandoned the rafts. Another portage was made, only this time it was an easy one, over a good trail.

At the bottom of the rapids, just as they were setting up camp, one of the men shouted out and pointed downstream. There was a canoe making its way toward them, paddled by four men. It was an unbelievable sight. Could it mean that Fort Kamloops was closer than they supposed?

The four strangers were prospectors. They said that they had been up as far as the Albreda earlier in the season and had found gold. It was coarse and heavy, but would say nothing more beyond that.

"How far is it to Fort Kamloops?" asked Augustus.

"About 200 miles," one of the strangers answered, "but it's good trail most of the way down."

Augustus nodded. He was skeptical of their estimate of the distance to the fort. The intelligence they had received was that it was only slightly more than 200 miles from the Cache to Kamloops. And did Cardinal himself not say, back at the headwaters, that it was only 170 from there? They must have come at least 70 miles since then, so surely the man was mistaken. They had to be within a hundred miles of their destination.

Rather than take the time to build more rafts, most of the party set out on foot. However, it was becoming increasingly difficult for Catherine to walk, so the Schuberts decided to stay on the river. Furthermore, the prospectors said it was safe the rest of the way and would not require any portages. The two farmhands from Fort Garry, André and Pierre, stayed with the family, and they all spent two more days building a raft and preparing themselves for what they hoped would be the final run to Fort Kamloops.

The foot-party was many miles downstream before the Schuberts finally got their raft launched. The river was painfully slow in places, but it at least ensured a safe journey. For the first time in weeks they could all rest a little. They drifted along, rowing when they needed to, and feeling generally secure from the elements. Even the rain had stopped and the air was warmer. But their food supplies were running ominously low. They were able to pot a game bird or two, but it was barely enough to keep them going. Then they ran out of ammunition, and their shotguns were rendered useless. Hunger stalked them. The children whined and complained, mostly because of their empty bellies, but partly because of their confinement to a small raft day after day. Catherine tried to entertain them as best she could by telling stories, but beyond that there was little she could do. As for herself, she was feeling all right, but was certain that her baby would be wanting its first glimpse of the world any day now.

Augustus snubbed the raft near an Indian village and he, André and Pierre went to see if they could barter for food. While procuring some potatoes from an old man, they heard Catherine yell from the river. Rushing back, they discovered an Indian woman trying to untie the raft and set it adrift with Catherine and the children still aboard. The woman indicated that the rawhide rope securing the raft had come from her cow that had recently been stolen. Augustus pantomimed that the rope belonged to him, and was from his cow, that he himself had killed. But the woman either didn't believe him or didn't understand him, so before serious trouble broke out, he and the farmhands jumped on board and pushed the raft away from the bank, quickly poling into deeper water. The exasperated woman was still gesticulating and muttering angrily as she receded in the distance.

The potatoes were gone in no time at all. The children got most of them, not only for the nourishment, but also to keep them from crying, the sound of which tore at Catherine's heart more than anything. Awful sounds like these had filled her ears as an adolescent in Ireland and she had prayed never to hear them again. Now they came from her own children, and she was devastated. She pleaded for Augustus to pull the raft into shore more often than he would have liked in an attempt to find food, but they came up with nothing.

At another Indian village they found everyone dead from smallpox. The corpse of a young man lay sprawled in the open, and they could see other bodies through the open doorways of the huts. The scene was ugly and filled them with revulsion, but not enough to quell the gnawing hunger in their bellies. They scoured the village for food like ravenous animals. In a garden behind the huts, they found a few potatoes, stuffed them in their shirts and pockets, and left as fast as they could. The potatoes lasted till the following morning, then all that was left to stave off starvation were the hips from wild rose bushes growing profusely in places along the shore.

The country was opening up, though, and that was a good sign. Ahead, Augustus could see a rampart of mountains running east and west, perpendicular to the valley of the North Thompson, and he was certain that that was where this river joined its southern branch. The prospectors back at the rapids had told him that it would be the best indication that they were nearing Fort Kamloops.

Before the confluence of the rivers was reached, Catherine's insides felt as if they were being squeezed by a giant hand. It was an old familiar feeling, instantly recognizable, and it was followed by a flow of water that soaked her undergarments. When she informed Augustus of this unnerving bit of news he immediately began looking for a suitable place to tie up. All Catherine could do was hope that the unstoppable forces at work in her lower abdomen would at least wait until she had reached dry land.

They saw smoke curling up from a smattering of Indian huts along the bank, and headed toward them. Before the raft even touched land André had leapt ashore and was running to see if there was a woman willing to help.

Meanwhile, Pierre secured the raft while Augustus assisted Catherine to shore. He spread a blanket on the ground and helped her lie down. "The baby is coming," she said. "It will wait no longer." She drew her knees up, her face contorted in pain, and suppressed a moan.

Augustus, having been through the procedure before, knew what to do. He threw back her dress and said, "Up with your bottom, Cath," and when Catherine lifted herself, he removed her bloomers. Now the contractions were tumbling over each other in intense waves of pain; Catherine groaned loudly, and Augustus placed a willow stick in her mouth for her to bite down on. Sweat broke out on her upper lip and brow. More pain now, and Augustus said he could see the baby — its head, thank God — with hair as black as the coal seams on the Pembina River.

Catherine screamed as she gave a mighty push, and the head was completely out. A final grunt and she was sure that her entire insides had slithered out into Augustus' waiting hands. He laid the baby down between Catherine's raised and parted legs, then stuck a callused finger into its mouth to clear out the mucous and to make sure its tongue was where it ought to be. There was another spasm, and another slithering of Catherine's insides as the placenta was expelled. A native woman arrived, and a ring of curious onlookers. The woman took a piece of rawhide decorating her dress, tied off the umbilical cord, then deftly sliced it through with a knife. Using some clean rags she had brought, she wiped the infant off, swaddled it, then gave the tiny thing to its mother. Not till then did the Schuberts realize that their fourth child was a girl.

"Cumloops," the native woman said, smiling, "Cumloops," and no one knew if she was referring to the fort, or whether she believed it would be a good name for the baby. Whatever the case, Catherine already knew her name. "She will be Rosa," she said, a child born in the wilds, whose parents' lives had been sustained by the hips of wild roses.

Later, Catherine was helped back to the raft, and the bite of the baby at her breast gave her a new-found strength. Augustus couldn't recall being this content since they had left Fort Garry an eon ago. Even his toothache had subsided. He pushed off from shore and soon they were rounding the point of land where the two rivers meld into one. The buildings of the fort, on the far shore, were a sight to behold, but then so were these vagabonds: four adults and four children, as bedraggled as paupers and thin as saplings, appearing on a log raft from out of the wilderness, into this small slice of civilization that represented life itself.[4] It was not a sight the settlement had ever seen before nor would ever see again. And it was Catherine, with her children, the baby at her breast, who made it so utterly extraordinary.

The Schuberts tied up at the small dock by the fort on October 14, four and half months after leaving Fort Garry, and six long weeks from Tête Jaune Cache. Over the last stage of their journey they had averaged less than five miles a day, and the ones that were easy could be tallied up on two hands. But they had done it; they had walked the tightrope to triumph while disaster lurked beside them every step of the way. And though the trek was far from over, the worst it had to offer was now at their backs. Like those who preceded them — the foot-party had arrived three days earlier, bedraggled, half-starved, but immensely pleased to be embraced once more by the arms of civilization, be it ever so modest — and the dozen or so who would arrive after them, they were a sorry-looking lot indeed, but alive, and not ungrateful for the miracle.

Epilogue

THE SCHUBERTS

The Schuberts spent the winter at Fort Kamloops, the chief factor putting Augustus to work as both a carpenter and a cook. When news came of the loss of Robertson and Pattison on the Fraser River, Catherine was heartbroken, but was immensely relieved to know that McMicking had reached the coast safe and sound.[1] In the spring of 1863 they moved to Lillooet and bought a parcel of farmland that Catherine worked while Augustus went up to Cariboo, as determined as ever to look for gold. Later, they moved to Clinton and started another farm. Each summer Augustus went into the Williams Creek area on his quest for gold, and though he did not find his fortune, he made enough to support his family and put a little aside. Meanwhile, since there were no schools in BC's interior, Catherine instructed her children, as well as many others in the district, at home. From 1877 to 1883 she was matron at the newly founded Cache Creek boarding school. She tended to the housekeeping, nursed children when they were ill and taught home economics, or "domestic science" as it is called today.

Augustus and Catherine Schubert.
(COURTESY OF THE FAMILY)

After 15 years the Schuberts bought land in the Spallumcheen Valley, a northern extension of the Okanagan Valley, and left Gus Jr. behind to work the farm in Clinton. Once she had settled in their new home, Catherine oversaw the planting of many fruit trees, for it was her contention that this valley, and even the Okanagan Valley, were prime orchard country.

For the next quarter-century Spallumcheen was the Schuberts' home, not far from their fellow overlander and friend, Alexander Fortune. Others who settled there would come to know the couple well, for both were quick to lend a hand whenever it was needed. What's more, the newcomers would come to know of the incredible journey made by the smiling, hard-working Irish woman and her equally industrious husband, and would give them their highest accolade. They would call them *overlanders*.

In 1908, at the age of 82, Augustus was up in his barn loft pitching feed down for his horses when he slipped and fell, breaking several ribs. He was too old to rally from the injuries and died a few days later. Catherine buried him on a hillside above the farm, in what is now Lansdowne Cemetery.

Ten years later, in her 83rd year, Catherine also passed away, peacefully, in bed, in her home, as she had wanted. She was laid to rest alongside Augustus, overlooking the valley both had come to love so well.

These days, to walk the streets of the town of Armstrong is to walk on what was once the Schubert farm. In 1926, the townsfolk erected a monument upon which is inscribed a picture of a Red River cart and these words: "In honour of Catherine Schubert who in company with her husband and three small children was a member of the hazardous overland expedition of 1862 across the Canadian Rockies from Fort Garry to Kamloops. A brave and notable pioneer."

Indeed.

THOMAS McMICKING

Despite seeing the disappointed faces of the miners streaming out of Williams Creek heading for the coast, McMicking set out for the diggings immediately after arriving at Quesnellemouth. He only got as far as Cottonwood House, some 17 miles along the road to the creek, before all the discouraging news he was hearing turned him around in his tracks. It was a difficult reality to accept after the monumental struggle he had had to get there, but it would not be denied. He followed in the footsteps of many of his fellow overlanders who had already gone to the coast, where things were cheaper and the climate warmer. He was elated when news filtered down to him that Catherine Schubert and her family had arrived safely in Fort Kamloops and that she had given birth to a healthy baby daughter, the first white child to be born in British Columbia's interior. Sadly, he never saw Catherine again. Neither did he see Sellar nor did he return to Cariboo.

McMicking made his home in New Westminster, and over the next few years busied himself with a variety of jobs, eventually accepting an appointment as the town clerk and assessor. He became an elder in the local Presbyterian church, the mighty Fraser having helped to reconcile his faith with his piety. No longer did he feel that he was he just going through the motions — he was a true believer again. He was also an active member around town on various boards and committees, and there were many who said his destiny lay in politics. Happily, he was able to bring Laura and the children out from Queenston, and in 1865 their fifth child was born.

In April of 1866 he was appointed deputy sheriff for the local district. In August he and Laura took the children to visit friends who lived by the Fraser River, about six miles below New Westminster.[2] While playing at the river's edge their six-year-old, son, Frank, fell in. Quick as a heartbeat, McMicking dove in to rescue the boy. The powerful current overwhelmed both father and son, and sucked them beneath a log boom. Both were drowned.

His funeral was of a size that the townsfolk of New Westminster had not seen before, and would not see again for years to come. Not only were they burying one of their leading citizens, they were burying an *overlander*, and more than that, the man who had *led* those stalwart people. Indeed, of all McMicking's positive attributes — and he had many — the ability to lead, with good judgment, fairness and intelligence, was one of his best. That he got the company from Fort Garry to Tête Jaune Cache, and kept them working reasonably well together for more than three months and a thousand miles of wilderness, was a remarkable feat of leadership, to say the least. When people recalled him in later years it would rarely be as a deputy sheriff, or as a city clerk or even a church elder. It would be as an *overlander*.

JAMES SELLAR

At Quesnellemouth, James Sellar sold his ox and tent for a profit and went south, working where he could along the way. Still a bundle of energy, at one roadhouse he cut 40 cords of wood in eight days for $100. When he arrived on the coast he could find no work in either New Westminster or Victoria, so on November 18, 1862, he was on a steamer bound for San Francisco. He returned to Cariboo in 1863, but had no luck and went home. An uncle died and left him some money, which he invested in a shoe-and-boot store in Toronto, but he soon tired of the business and sold it. His restless spirit took him to North Dakota where he turned to farming. He died an old man in Minneapolis, the place he'd set out from on foot so many years before on the adventure of a lifetime. Perhaps that was one of the reasons he returned there.

James Sellar was unquestionably narrow-minded, but his anti-Catholic sentiments were not untypical for the times. He was also certainly the human dynamo of the overlanders. No doubt his boundless enthusiasm and energy were an annoyance to many people during the initial stages of the journey, particularly his drive to be the first to move out every morning and therefore have his pick of the best campsites at night. But as the trip wore on, and as the energy and spirit of the company flagged, he was precisely what it needed.

Alexander Fortune

At Quesnellemouth, Fortune's goal was still the goldfields and there was no way he was going to the coast without seeing them, despite the negative news. Besides, what was another 50 or 60 miles to someone who had just walked 20 times that? He set off with James Wattie on foot, through the rain and mud. Following behind him like a puppy was the ox he had purchased back in Fort Garry. Fortune was the only overlander to have retained his original animal and it had come to mean something more to him than a beast of burden or a future meal. At the diggings, the overlanders soon discovered that they had a greater chance of being struck by lightning during an April shower than of finding gold. Not only was there not much ground left on which to stake a claim, most of the claims weren't producing anything but backaches and heartaches.

Returning to Quesnellemouth, he and Wattie met a man who had come from Victoria by an unconventional route. Instead of using either the Yale or Lillooet routes, he had come via Bella Coola, an Indian village 200 miles west of Quesnellemouth, at the head of Bentinck Arm, an inlet of the Pacific Ocean. After weighing all the possibilities they decided to try this route. Joined by James Wattie's brother, William, they built a raft and sailed downstream to Fort Alexandria, then headed west into the mountains on foot. Fortune's beloved ox was still tagging along behind. The men shot game birds to supplement their rations, and near Puntzi Lake met up with a band of Chilcotin Indians who kindly invited them to dinner. A wolf was cooked up and was so foul that the taste of it stayed with the men for months afterwards. William Wattie would never see a dog again without being reminded of that meal.

Farther down the trail their food supply ran out and their ammunition was down to one bullet. James brought down a duck with it. Luckily, a pack train bound for Quesnellemouth happened along and the men were able to replenish their supplies. At a meadow they met some men cutting hay for the pack train on its return trip, and Fortune decided to leave his ox there.[3] He did so with great reluctance for he had become quite attached to the animal. However, he was advised that there would be no feed for it beyond this point, particularly on the coast, and the animal would surely starve. He told the men he would get it the next time he was through this way, if he ever was.[4]

Reaching the Bella Coola River, the overlanders hired Indians to take them to Bentinck Arm by canoe, another 30 miles downstream. The river was rough and full of snags, and a canoe preceding them, loaded with eight Indians, some of whom were drunk, overturned. Five were drowned.

The Indian village at Bella Coola was decimated by smallpox. There were dead bodies in the woods around the encampment. The men heard a baby's cry coming from a bush and found an infant, black with the pox, left there to die.

They had expected that a crew would be at Bella Coola, ready to begin construction of the road to Fort Alexandria, and that they would obtain work, but there was no one around. After waiting three weeks for a steamer to arrive, they grew impatient and engaged Indians to canoe them the 70 miles to Bella Bella, closer to the open ocean. From there they persuaded other Indians to take them to Port Hardy on Vancouver Island, a longer paddle of more than a hundred miles, some of it over the exposed waters of Queen Charlotte Strait.[5] They waited three more weeks at the fort before they boarded a steamer bound for Victoria, where they arrived some time in late November.

In Victoria, Fortune opened the Overland Restaurant with Bill Morrow, but eventually returned to Williams Creek. Finding nothing but a lot of experience, he went to Big Bend on the Columbia River, where the next big strike was supposed to happen. It never did. He ended his years as a farmer in the Spallumcheen Valley, teaching the local natives the tenets of Christianity. He died in 1915, and was buried in Lansdowne Cemetery, a few feet away from his old friend Augustus Schubert.

THE OTHERS

Like the main characters, the minor ones went in a variety of directions after the journey.

James Wattie mined in Cariboo for a couple of years, initially on the claim of his old friend John "Cariboo" Cameron, one of the few miners to actually strike it rich, and then on his own claim which was adjacent to Cameron's.[6] He did not find his Eldorado and returned east in 1864. For many years he operated a woollen mill in Valleyfield, Quebec, and died in 1907.

William Wattie worked with his brother in Cariboo, then also went home where he was a machinist in the weaving industry. At his death in 1917, he held 60 patents on devices used in that industry.

John Fannin, who scrambled to safety on a rock in the North Thompson River, mined in Cariboo without much luck either, but eventually became renowned for his interest in natural history and the many papers he wrote on the subject. He helped found the B.C. Provincial Museum, and several geographical features are named after him.

William Hugill, who was stranded with Fannin on the North Thompson, made it to Williams Creek. He died from an illness in 1863, at the age of 25, and is buried in the Barkerville cemetery. More than a century passed before his family found out his fate: they saw his headstone on a CBC television show.

Archibald Thompson, the third member of the stranded party, became a bridge superintendent in the east and died in 1909. William Fortune, the fourth member, settled in Tranquille, BC, and his home was eventually turned into a sanatorium. He died in 1914 and is buried in Kamloops.

Dr. Eady Stevenson, who tended to Bill Morrow when the ox cart ran over him, practised medicine in various places in the west, and ended up in Victoria where he died in 1909.

Peter Marlow, who was so helpful with the Schuberts' children, ended up back in Canada West with seven children of his own. He died in 1912 and is buried in Grimsby, Ontario.

Michel Callihoo eventually settled on a reserve northwest of Edmonton. A chief, he died in 1910.

Dobson Prest, the man who tried to stop the ox cart from running over William Morrow, ended up in Truckee, Nevada, where he died in 1885. But Morrow, Andrew Holes, (the man who rescued John Fannin from the rock), James Kelso (who nearly drowned in the South Saskatchewan River), George Wonnacott (who was stuck in the swamp), the guides Charles Racette and André Cardinal, and the Schuberts' farmhands André and Pierre, all drifted into obscurity.

Author's Note

Several different parties, besides McMicking's, made the trek overland between Fort Garry and the goldfields. I have taken events from some of those other parties and assigned them to characters in the McMicking party. This was done for the sake of brevity, and to avoid confusing the reader with too many names, as well as to offer a flavour of what all the groups experienced. Also, though some of the thoughts of the main characters are on record (e.g., Sellar's anti-Catholic views) I have given them thoughts that they may or may not have had but are, I think, consistent with the sort of people they were. Except for these embellishments, the McMicking party's journey unfolded pretty much the way it has been presented in the preceding pages.

For those who want the full details, I recommend Richard Thomas Wright's thoroughly researched book *Overlanders*.

One final note: In his epilogue (page 250) Wright laments: "Generally the Overlanders are remarkable in our lack of familiarity, our lack of memorials. Where are the markers for the ten dead Overlanders? Where the marker for Slaughter Camp, or the Tête Jaune Camp or the numerous prairie camps?"

Well, where are they? We have a Redcoat Trail, marking the Mounties' foray into the West; why don't we have an Overlander Trail? After all, they preceded the Mounties by a dozen years. If it was marked with cairns and plaques, and the occasional campsite and rest area along the way, what a wonderful "hands-on" history lesson it would be. If that's too grandiose a scheme, I believe Wright has suggested a good place to start giving these remarkable people the recognition they deserve. He thinks he's pinpointed the location of Slaughter Camp which, he says, could be proved or disproved with some archaeological work. As far as archaeological digs go, it would probably be basic and inexpensive. So what are we waiting for?

Endnotes

PROLOGUE

1 In his reminiscences, James Schubert wrote that the Indians were also on the run. Apparently they had massacred some settlers, and were being chased by soldiers.

THE ROAD TO FORT GARRY

1 This marked the beginning of the Sioux War, a part of which was the attack on the stage near Georgetown. It might have been averted if the Americans had kept their promises to the Sioux of exchanging land for food. Instead, when a chief complained that his people were starving, he was told by an agent that if his people were hungry, they should eat grass. It was the spark that ignited the war. By the time it was over, several hundred white settlers and soldiers were dead and many women and children were kidnapped. The agent himself was found dead, his mouth stuffed with grass.

THE ROAD TO FORT EDMONTON

1 In 1857 the livestock consisted of approximately 2,800 horses, 2,700 oxen, 6,000 cattle including calves, 4,700 pigs, and 2,500 sheep. (*Narrative of the Canadian Red River Exploring Expedition of 1857.* p. 228)

2 No other cart trains made the long trek, and the railroad wasn't completed until 1885.

3 A census taken in 1856 showed 534 Catholic families and 548 Protestant families consisting of 488 Episcopalians and 60 Presbyterians. (*Narrative of the Canadian Red River Exploring Expedition of 1857.* p. 195)

4 The spring democrat wagon was basically a shallow box with two to four seat-boards. Each seat would hold two people, but one or all of the boards could be removed so that the vehicle could be used to haul supplies. The box was mounted on springs, which made the ride more comfortable and, unlike the carts, the wagon had four wheels. The name "democrat" came from the vehicle's plain and democratic character.

5 Known to the overlanders as the Scratching River.

6 James Bird Jr. a.k.a "Jamey Jock" and "Jimmy." Born around 1798, Bird was the son of an HBC chief factor and was apprenticed when he was 11 years old. He worked for both the HBC and the American Fur Trade Company who both suspected his loyalty. He is best remembered for his work as an interpreter on the treaty with the Blackfeet in 1877. He died in 1892.

7 While it was true that attitudes toward sex and drinking in the settlement were much more liberal than the men had been accustomed to, and that some took advantage of this fact, McMicking's attitude was typical of the hypocrisy paramount during the Victorian era when private lives were often scandalously different from their public façade.

8 The Reverend may very well have typified Victorian hypocrisy. A married man, he apparently took advantage of his Metis servant girl at every opportunity. When she became pregnant, he tried aborting the fetus himself. When it didn't work, his nefarious deeds were soon discovered, and six months later he was sent to jail for them. He proclaimed his innocence, stating that the HBC had framed him because he had once publicly spoken out against the Company. His supporters in the community got up a petition to have him freed, and when it didn't work, stormed the fort's jail and freed him themselves.

9 James McKay, also known as "Big Jim" (for good reason — he tipped the scales at 364 pounds) was a well-respected guide who, among other things, had taken John Palliser on his journey of discovery in 1857, and Governor George Simpson on his first foray into Rupert's Land from St. Paul in 1859. He did the same for Governor Dallas and was with him in Georgetown when the overlanders were there. The overlanders would have loved to have him as their guide, but he was not available.

10 This was an HBC post set up for the surrounding Métis farms and was about five miles beyond the present town of St. Francois–Xavier.

11 When the Boundary Commission was establishing the border between Canada and the United States in 1875, one of the men on the survey crew carelessly scraped a match on his boot and a spark from it ignited the grass. The resulting fire spread as far south as the Missouri River, 150 miles to the south.

12 A conservative estimate of deaths during the "Great Hunger" in Ireland is 800,000. It may have been more than a million. Those who didn't die

of starvation died of contagious diseases, which spread swiftly across a land devastated by so much misery and grief that it was beyond human comprehension. It precipitated a mass exodus of a million people, many of whom died on the "coffin ships" to North America.

13 James Sellar, Diary.

14 During the summer of 1860, Jean Gravelet (Blondin), a Frenchman, and William Hunt (Signor Farini), a Canadian, mesmerized thousands of onlookers as they tried to outdo each other on both tight and slack ropes across the Niagara River. Blondin once carried his manager across, piggyback, and Signor Farini walked half way across, then descended on a 200-foot rope to the *Maid of the Mist*, drank a glass of wine, climbed back up, and continued on to the far side.

15 Pronounced "shimsa." An Irish-Gaelic word for a party of song and dance.

16 James Sellar, Diary.

17 The Company obviously didn't put any of this profit back into maintaining the scow. When Walter Cheadle and Viscount Milton came through on their epic journey to the west coast some three months later, the scow was filled with water and the bottom logs were floating. One of their group boarded with two horses and it promptly sank to the bottom.

18 Though none of the Americans reached the Fraser River goldfields, they all crossed the Rockies safely in the dead of winter, despite Racette's desertion.

19 Ultimately the buffalo bones scattered across the southern Canadian prairie did not go to waste. Their value was soon realized and "bone pickers" collected and sold them to companies that converted them to, among other things, fertilizer. When the railroad came, stations had mountainous piles of bones collected for pick-up. South of the border, at the peak of the buffalo slaughter, a bone mound 12 feet high, stretched for a half mile along the track.

20 The spot where the overlanders crossed is at the National Historic Site of Batoche, where the last battle of the Riel Rebellion was fought in 1885. It is still possible to walk down the trail, through the trees, to the river's edge.

21 James Sellar, Diary.

22 Henry Wadsworth Longfellow, "The Day is Done," 1845.

23 Visitors to Fort Edmonton today will find it on the south bank of the river, but it is only a replica. The fort the overlanders came to was a few miles downstream on the north side, approximately where the Legislative Buildings are.

THE ROAD TO TÊTE JAUNE CACHE

1 McMicking was wrong. It was actually a coal seam that had indeed been burning for years, and would go on burning for several more.

2 Known then as the Buffalo Dung River. "Lobstick" refers to the trees trimmed to mark the trail, or to mark a special spot. All but the uppermost limbs were "lobbed" off so that the tree looked like a stick with a few branches on top.

3 Known as the Carrot River.

4 Ten years later, the inscription was still there, though partly obliterated. Sandford Fleming came across it during his surveying expedition in September 1872.

5 Known as the Prairie River.

6 James Sellar, Diary.

7 In the early 20th century, the house was torn down by railway surveyors who used its timbers to make a raft.

8 Now the Yellowhead Pass.

9 The overlanders thought the two lakes were one — Cow Dung Lake.

10 When the overlanders came through Tête Jaune Cache, it was situated three or four miles downstream from where the present community sits near the junction of Highways 16 and 5. The original site no longer exists, having been long covered over by the Fraser River.

11 Essentially, the area between Kamloops and Sicamous, BC.

THE ROAD TO CARIBOO

1 The present town of Quesnel was then called Quesnellemouth, to distinguish it from Quesnelle Forks, at the confluence of the Quesnel and Cariboo rivers.

2 Cottonwood Canyon, a few miles above Quesnel.

THE ROAD TO FORT KAMLOOPS

1 Known as Canoe Mountain.

2 The distance from this point (Slaughter Camp) to Tête Jaune Cache was paced off by Alfred Selwyn during his surveying trip in 1871 and reckoned to be 78 miles rather than 60.

3 The exact location of Slaughter Camp is not known, but author Richard Thomas Wright found a grove of cedar and hemlock trees, north of Blue River, among which were many ancient stumps, that he thinks might

have been the camp.

4 Though an HBC fort, Kamloops lacked the palisades that typified most of the Company's other forts. Indian-white relations in the valley were amicable, making protective walls unnecessary.

EPILOGUE

1 In addition to the deaths of Alexander Robertson, Eustache Pattison and William Strachan, Frank Penwarden of the North Thompson party drowned in rapids below Kamloops Lake. A later party rafting the Fraser lost two men, Philip Leader and James Carpenter. (Ironically Carpenter had made an entry in his diary on the day of his death that read "Arrived this day at the canyon at 10 a.m. and drowned running the canoe down. God keep my poor wife.") The Rennie party, the last to come through that year, lost two men to cannibalism.

2 The natural presumption would be the North Arm of the Fraser, and near Boundary Road, the street that separates Vancouver from the municipality of Burnaby.

3 The pack train never returned. Two days later it was ambushed by the same band of Indians that had fed the overlanders a meal of wolf meat. All the men were killed.

4 Not long after Fortune and the Watties left the meadow a group of half-starved miners arrived, so desperate for food that they killed the ox. They gave the hay-cutter $85, instructing him to make sure it got to the rightful owner. It took almost two years, but Fortune eventually got his money.

5 Known as Fort Rupert.

6 The Cameron story is legendary. Before he made his big strike his wife died, eliciting a promise from him on her deathbed not to bury her in Cariboo but to take her home to Glengarry County, in eastern Ontario. In the dead of winter, Cameron and his partner, Robert Stevenson, pulled the dead woman's coffin on a sled nearly 600 miles to the coast, risking life and limb in the process. He buried her temporarily in Victoria, then came back when he could afford it, exhumed her body, and took her home.

Bibliography

PUBLISHED SOURCES

Alexander, Richard Henry. *The Diary and Narrative of Richard Henry Alexander in a Journey Across the Rocky Mountains*, Introduction by Neil Brearly, Alcuin Society, Richmond, BC, 1973.

Butler, William Francis. *The Great Lone Land,* M.G. Hurtig Ltd., Edmonton, 1968.

Campbell, Marjorie Wilkins. *The Saskatchewan,* Clarke, Irwin & Co. Ltd., Toronto, 1982.

Cavell, Edward. *Journeys to the Far West,* James Lorimer and Company, Publishers, Toronto, ON, 1979.

Dary, David A. *The Buffalo Book: The Saga of an American Symbol,* Avon Books, New York, 1975.

Dunford, Muriel Poulton. *North River: The Story of British Columbia's North Thompson Valley & Yellowhead Highway 5,* Sonotek Publishing Ltd., Merritt, BC, 2000.

Hind, Henry Youle. *Narrative of the Canadian Red River Exploring Expedition of 1857 and of the Assiniboine and Saskatchewan Exploring Expedition of 1858,* M.G. Hurtig Ltd., Edmonton, 1971.

Hodgson, Barbara. *In the Arms of Morpheus,* Douglas & McIntyre Ltd., Vancouver, BC, 2001.

McMicking, Thomas. *Overland from Canada to British Columbia,* University of British Columbia Press, Vancouver, BC, 1981.

Newman, Peter C. *Caesars of the Wilderness,* Penguin Books, Markham, ON, 1987.

Wade, Mark S. *The Overlanders of '62,* Heritage House Publishing Co., Surrey, BC, 1981.

Wallace, Martin. *A Short History of Ireland,* David & Charles Ltd., Great Britain, 1978.

Wright, Richard Thomas. *Overlanders,* Western Producer Prairie Books, Saskatoon, Saskatchewan, 1985.

_____. *Yellowhead Mileposts: Points of Interest Along a Famous Road,* Vol. 1, Mitchell Press, Vancouver, BC, 1974.

UNPUBLISHED SOURCES

Fortune, A.L. "Reminiscences," EE F77, British Columbia Archives.

Redgrave, S. "Overland Journey to British Columbia in 1862," EB R24, British Columbia Archives.

Schubert, James. "Reminiscences," EE Sch7, British Columbia Archives.

Sellar, James. "Diary, April 22, 1862 – Nov. 22, 1862," EB Se4, British Columbia Archives.

Index